Natural Appearances, Natural Liberation

A Nyingma Meditative Guide
on the Six Bardos of Living and Dying

Master Tam Shek-wing

Translated by
Samten Migdron

With a foreword by
Tulku Thondup Rinpoche

SUMERU

NATURAL APPEARANCES, NATURAL LIBERATION
A Nyingma Meditative Guide on the Six Bardos of Living and Dying
Master Tam Shek-wing

Translated by Samten Migdron
Edited by Sandra Monteath
Designed by Karma Yonten Gyatso
Front cover: Karma Lingpa thangka, photographed by Ed Lui
Back cover & page 16: Master Tam Shek-wing, photographed by Fraser Shein

Published by
The Sumeru Press Inc.
PO Box 2089, Richmond Hill, ON
Canada L4E 1A3

CATALOGUING IN PUBLICATION DATA

Tam, Shek-wing
    Natural appearances, natural liberation : a Nyingma meditative guide on the six bardos of living and dying / Tam Shek-wing ; translated by Samten Migdron ; foreword by Thondup Tulku.

ISBN 978-1-896559-10-0

    1. Rñi·n-ma-pa (Sect)--Doctrines. 2. Rñi·n-ma-pa (Sect)--Rituals--Texts. 3. Buddhist literature, Tibetan. I. Title.

BQ7662.4.T36 2011   294.3'420423   C2011-904042-5

For more information about The Sumeru Press
visit us at *www.sumeru-books.com*

Contents

Foreword, by Tulku Thondup 7
      The *Profound Dharma of Natural Liberation* and Karma Lingpa
      The Six Bardos
      Lineage

Part I
Introduction to Fundamental Concepts
Related to Natural Liberation

1   To Undress Our Minds: The Illusory Nature of Cyclic Existence . . . 17

2   Liberating our Minds from the Cycle of Living and Dying 21

3   Experiencing the Cycle of Living and Dying
    in One Meditation Session 25
      The Six Realms
      Meditation Practice (1)
      Meditation Practice (2)

4   Understanding the Concept of Naturally Arisen Phenomena 31
      Naturally Arisen Phenomena
      Primordial Ground
      The Emptiness of All Phenomena

5   Natural Liberation and *Tathagatagarbha* 38
      Natural Liberation through Recognizing the Nucleus of
         Enlightenment
      What is Natural Liberation?
      Parallel Teachings of Two Buddhist Texts

6   The Six Bardos 44
      The Six Bardos
      The Three Pairs

Part II
The Practice Instructions of the Six Bardos

7   Practice Instruction for the Bardo of Living (Part 1) 51
        "A Pigeon Returning to Its Nest" – The Realization of
            Primordial Abode
        Illusory World
        Meditation Practice
        The Natural Liberation of the Foundation

8   Practice Instruction for the Bardo of Living (Part 2) 57
        Seven-point Posture of Vairocana
        Simple Meditation Practice
        Stone Gazing
        Proper Breathing

9   Practice Instruction for the Bardo of Living (Part 3) 63
        Meditation on Holy Beings
        Tranquility Meditation without Signs
        Insight Meditation
        Recognizing the Mind-Itself
        Searching for the Mind-Itself
        Ascertaining the Nature of Primordial Awareness or *Rigpa*

10   Practice Instruction for the Bardo of Dreams (Part 1) 73
        The Daytime Practice of Illusory Body, Speech and Mind
        The Practice of Pure Illusory Body

11   Practice Instruction for the Bardo of Dreams (Part 2) 80
        Apprehending the Dream State
        Emanation and Transformation
        The Four Dispersals

12   Practice Instruction for the Bardo of Dreams (Part 3) 89
        What is the Clear Light of Purity?
        Clear Light of Sleep
        Clear Light of Death

Clear Light of Guru and Clear Light of *Bindu*
The Practice Instruction on Attaining the Mind of Clear Light –
    The Clear Light of Awareness

13 Threefold Space and the Four Liberations – The Bardo of Meditation 98
    Threefold Space Meditation
    Moheyan and the Tibetans
    The Four Liberations

14 The Bardo of Dying (Part 1) 109
    Liberation through the Transfer of Consciousness
    The Tibetan Book of the Dead
    Further Adaptations

15 The Bardo of Dying (Part 2) 117
    The Signs of Death
    Signs of Death According to the Vajrayana
    The Four Dissolutions
    The Clear Light of Death
    How to Abide in the Clear Light of Death

16 The Bardo of Dying (Part 3) 127
    The Practice and Actual Undertaking of Transference of
        Consciousness
    The Nine Apertures
    The Upper Three Apertures
    The Middle Three Apertures
    The Lower Three Apertures
    Meditation of Body
    Meditation of Wind
    Meditation of Mind
    Dharmakaya Transference
    Sambhogakaya Transference
    Nirmanakaya Transference
    Mundane Transference

17 The Bardo of *Dharmata* (Part 1) 138
       Fear and Away From Fear

18 The Bardo of *Dharmata* (Part 2) 146
       The Arising of The Four Visions
       The Vision of Direct Realization of Ultimate Nature
       The Vision of the Increase of Experience
       The Vision of the Perfection of Intrinsic Awareness
       The Vision of Cessation into Ultimate Nature

19 The Bardo of Becoming (Part 1) 155
       "Opening Up a Blocked Water Channel by Joining It With
            Another Channel"
       Mental Body and Body of Habitual Tendencies

20 The Bardo of Becoming (Part 2) 163
       Six Ways of Blocking the Entrance of the Womb
            With our Personal Deity
            With our Spiritual Guru and his Consort
            By Generating the Four (States of) Bliss
            With the Antidote of Renunciation
            With the Clear Light
            With the Illusory Body

21 Conclusion – The Three States of Meditative Absorption 170

Translator's Postscript 177

Foreword

The *Profound Dharma of Natural Liberation through the Intention of the Peaceful and Wrathful Ones* (Tib. *Zab chos zhi khro dgongs pa rang grol*)[1] is a cycle of profound esoteric ritual texts and meditations on the peaceful and wrathful deities in the Nyingma (Tib. *rNying ma*) school of Tibetan Buddhism. The cycle reveals how to apply both the divine forms and the wisdom, that is, the pure quality and nature of the body and mind, as the forty-two peaceful (Tib. *zhi*) and fifty-eight wrathful (Tib. *khro*) deities.

The *Profound Dharma of Natural Liberation* and Karma Lingpa

The *Profound Dharma of Natural Liberation* was discovered as a hidden treasure text (Tib. *gter ma*)[2] by Karma Lingpa (Tib. *Karma Gling pa*), one of the greatest discoverers, or *terton* (Tib. *gter ston*), of mystical teachings. In the ninth century, Tibetans benefitted from a 55-year-long visit to their land by Guru

---

1 Sources for this foreword:
1) *Zab chos zhi khro dgongs pa rang grol gyi them byang: zin bris*, ff. 1-6, in *Zhi khro dgongs pa rang grol gyi chos skor* Vol. I. (Pub. by Sherab Lama, 1975-76).
2) *Zab chos zhi khro dgongs pa rang grol gyi brgyud pa'i lo rgyus mdor bsdus nor bu'i phreng ba* by Rgya ra ba Nam mkha' chos kyi rgya mtsho, ff. 27-48, in *Zhi khro dgongs pa rang grol gyi chos skor* Vol. I. Vol. I. (Pub. by Sherab Lama, 1975-76).
3) *Zab chos zhi khro dgongs pa rang grol las: smin byed sgo 'byed dbang bskur 'bring po 'gro drug rang grol la kha bskong phyag bzhes kyis brgyan pa 'brel tshad rang grol* by 'Jam mgon Kong sprul, ff. 145-228, in *Zhi khro dgongs pa rang grol gyi chos skor* Vol. II. Vol. II. (Pub. by Sherab Lama, 1975-76).
4) *Zab chos zhi khro dgongs pa rang grol las: bar do'i smon lam rnam gsum*, ff. 315-327, in *Zhi khro dgongs pa rang grol gyi chos skor* Vol. III. (Pub. by Sherab Lama, 1975-76).
5) *Bstan pa'i snying po gsang chen snga 'gyur nges don zab mo'i chos kyi byung ba gsal bar byed pa'i legs bshad mkhas pa dga 'byed ngo mtshar gtam gyi rol mtso* by Guru Bkra shis, f. 457 (Pub. by Krung bod kyi shes rig dpe bskrun khang, 1990).
6) *Zab mo'i gter dang gter ston grub thob ji ltar byong pa'i lo rgyus rin po che baidurya'i phreng ba* by Kong sprul Yon tan rgyal mtsho, f. 24a/3 (Pub. by Ngodrup and Sherab Drimed, 1977).
7) *Gangs ljongs rgyal ba'i bstan pa rin po che ji ltar byung ba'i tshul dag ching gsal bar bkod pa lha dbang gyul las rgyal ba'i rnga bo che' i sgra dbyangs* by 'Jigs bral ye shes rdo rje, f. 289b/2 (Pub. by Dudjom Rinpoche, 1967).

2 On "gter" and "gter ston", see: *Las 'phro gter brgyud kyi rnam bshad nyung gsal ngo mtshar rgya mtsho* by 'Jigs med bstan pa'i nyi ma (Pub. by Dodrupchen Rinpoche, 1974); Tulku Thondup, *Hidden Teachings of Tibet* (Boston: Wisdom Publications, 1997).

Padmasambhava, one of the greatest enlightened masters in Buddhist history and the founder of Buddhism in Tibet. At his disciples' request, Guru Padmasambhava condensed the inner esoteric teachings and wisdom of Buddhism in the form of the *Profound Dharma of Natural Liberation*. Then through the power of his wisdom-mind, he concealed (Tib. *sbas*) and entrusted (Tib. *gtad rgya*) the teachings and realizations of the *Profound Dharma of Natural Liberation* to the enlightened-nature of the minds of King Trisong Deutsen (Tib. *Khri srong lde btsan*, 790-958) of Tibet, the King's sons and the famed translator Chog-ro Lu-gyaltsen (Tib. *lCog ro Klu'i rgyal mtshan*). Thereafter, Guru Padmasambhava encoded the *Profound Dharma of Natural Liberation* in dakini symbolic scripts (Tib. *brda yig*) on a yellow scroll (Tib. *shog ser*) and concealed it at Daglha Gampo (Tib. *Dwags lha sgam po*) in Central Tibet.

In the fourteenth century, Chog-ro Lu-gyaltsen took rebirth as Karma Lingpa in Dagpo (Tib. *Dwags po*) valley in Central Tibet. Karma Lingpa's father was an adept known as Nyida Sangye (Tib. *Nyi zla sangs rgyas*). At the tender age of 15, Karma Lingpa discovered many profound treasure teachings from a "dancing angel-like"[3] hill behind Daglha Gampo,[4] among them was the yellow scroll that contained the symbolic scripts of the *Profound Dharma of Natural Liberation*. By his decoding the symbolic scripts, the teachings and realizations of the *Profound Dharma of Natural Liberation* were instantly awakened in Karma Lingpa, just as if he had learned and experienced them a moment ago. He then transcribed the decoded teachings in the form of texts. After a year or so, Karma Lingpa transmitted the complete cycle of the *Profound Dharma of Natural Liberation* to his small son, Nyida Choje (Tib. *Nyi zla chos rje*), and, following the instructions in "the prophetic guide" (Tib. *kha byang/ gter lung*) of the *Profound Dharma of Natural Liberation* itself, advised him to keep the transmission of the teachings restricted to a single-person lineage for three generations. Then, although he was still in his youth, Karma Lingpa died.

Nyida Choje transmitted the *Profound Dharma of Natural Liberation* to Nyida Odzer (Tib. *Nyi zla 'od zer*), who in turn transmitted it to Namkha Chokyi Gyatso (Tib. *Nam mkha chos kyi rgya mtsho*), who finally promulgated it to a larger audience through many lineages. Thereafter, the *Profound Dharma of Natural Liberation* became one of the most popular texts in the Nyingmapa world of Tibet and it remains so. In addition to Nyingmapas, many great teachers and

---

3   *Zab chos zhi khro dgongs pa rang grol gyi them byang: zin bris*, f. 5, in *Zhi khro dgongs pa rang grol gyi chos skor*, Vol. I (Pub. by Sherab Lama, 1975-76).

4   Daglha Gampo had become a famous place as it was the seat of one of the three most important teachers of the Kagyu (Tib. *bKa' brgyud*) school, the Lord Gamopopa (Tib. *sGam po pa*, "the one from sGam po," 1079-1153).

monasteries of the Kagyu school also practise the teachings.

In Eastern Tibet where I was born, the *Profound Dharma of Natural Liberation* was known as the *Thotol* (Tib. *thos grol*, "liberation by hearing"). It was one of the first major liturgical texts that novices study, not necessarily in order to learn its meaning, but to prepare to recite and chant at ceremonies. For advanced meditators who had studied the three inner *tantras* of the Nyingma school, the *Profound Dharma of Natural Liberation* was one of the standard *sadhana* texts used for putting their knowledge into practice and meditation.

The teachings of the *Profound Dharma of Natural Liberation* embody the essence of the three inner *tantras*: its teachings on the development stages (Tib. *bskyed pa*) embody the essence of Mahayoga teachings, such as the *Guhyagarbhatantra*; its teaching on the mandala of deities in the body (Tib. *lus dkyil*) and on the naturally liberated great bliss (Tib. *bde chen rang grol*) embodies the essence of Anuyoga teachings; its teachings on six bardos and six lights (Tib. *sgron ma drug*) embody the essence of Atiyoga.

The Six Bardos

The *Profound Dharma of Natural Liberation*, particularly those portions included in this volume, are the teachings on the bardo (Tib. *bar do*). Bardo means intermediate state or transitional state in Tibetan. In common parlance, bardo denotes the period between this life and the next. But here, bardo teachings apply to every transitional phase of life according to the essence of esoteric Buddhism. This includes life, death and after death; in short, every intermediate state and transitional moment. Further, different bardo states are either states of realization of the truth-as-it-is, or deluded states of the confused minds of ordinary beings. Therefore, teachings on bardo relate to every part of life.

The *tantras*[5] and other Nyingma texts contain teachings on four bardos: the bardo of living (Tib. *skye gnas*), the bardo of dying (Tib. *'chi'i kha*), the bardo of universal ultimate nature or *dharmata* (Tib. *chos nyid*) and the bardo of becoming (Tib. *srid pa*), which is the state between death and rebirth.

However, in the *Profound Dharma of Natural Liberation*, the essence of esoteric Buddhism is presented in the form of teachings on six bardos. The text says,

---

5   See the following *tantras* of rNying ma rgyud bum. (Pub. by Dilgo Khentse Rinpoche):
     rDzogs pa rang byung chen po, f. 1, vol. *ta*;
     Nyi zla kha sbyor, f. 386, vol. *ta*;
     Rig pa rang shur chen po, f. 1, vol. *tha*; and
     sGra thal 'gyur chen po, f. 386, vol. *tha*.

> In accordance with *The Seventeen Tantras* of the Great
> Perfection (Tib. *rdzogs pa chen po*) ... Guru Padmasambhava
> brought together the innermost essence of all the teachings by
> codifying all phenomenal existence as the six bardos. He named
> them the *Profound Dharma of Natural Liberation through the
> Intention of the Peaceful and Wrathful Ones* and concealed them
> as a *gter* in the dancing angel-like hill behind Daglha Gampo.[6]

The teachings on six bardos are as follows. The first is the meditative instructions for taking the bardo of living, our present transitional life, as the path of meditation. By focusing on learning, analyzing and meditating on tranquility (*shamatha*) and insight (*vipassana*), which is the recognition of intrinsic awareness, the practitioner trains on the path of realization of the mind and the appearances as the three Buddha bodies. Second is the teachings on the bardo of dreams (Tib. *rmi lam*). Through unwavering mindfulness, the practitioner trains on recognizing the dream, or delusion, and transforming it into luminous absorption. Third is the teachings on the bardo of meditation (luminous absorption) (Tib. *bsam gtan l'od gsal*). Through a meditative state in which there is no wavering, grasping and limit, the practitioner attains confidence in the four freedoms or four liberated states: primordially liberated state, self-liberated state, directly liberated state and totally liberated state. Fourth is the teachings on the bardo of dying, which explain the transference of consciousness at the time of dying or *phowa* (Tib. *'pho ba*). Any of the four methods of transference of consciousness brings about the transference of our unborn intrinsic awareness into the ultimate sphere, or, through the right aperture, our mind to a pure land. Fifth is the teachings on the bardo of *dharmata*, the true nature of the mind and phenomena. Through the training on the "four visions" (Tib. *snang ba bzhi*) the practitioner realizes all that arises is the natural appearance of the intrinsic awareness itself. Sixth is the teachings on the bardo of becoming, the state between death and rebirth. These focus on the spiritual methods for recognizing that we have died, sealing the apertures of rebirth in inferior realms, opening the path of rebirth in higher realms or pure lands and awakening higher stages of spiritual realization.

Through the training on the six bardos, a practitioner of high potential could attain liberation in this very bardo of living, a mediocre practitioner in the bardo of dying and an inferior one at the time of the bardo of *dharmata*. At the very least, training on the six bardos could lead a practitioner to the path of liberation

---

6   *Zab chos zhi khro dgongs pa rang grol gyi them byang: zin bris*, f. 5, in *Zhi khro dgongs pa rang grol gyi chos skor*, Vol. I (Pub. by Sherab Lama, 1975-76).

in the bardo of becoming.

The *Profound Dharma of Natural Liberation* is one of the major liturgical texts used for death rites in the Nyingma tradition. It provides a detailed meditative rite to purify the negative karmic effects or habits that the deceased could be harbouring within. It provides detailed meditative training on the pure forms, sounds and experiences of the peaceful and wrathful deities and their Buddha fields. If a practitioner perfects such training, he or she will be able to transform the frightening or alluring forms, sounds and feelings of the bardo of *dharmata*, which are all illusions of the mind, into Buddha forms and qualities. Then even if any negative image or sound should arise before him or her, what arises will only become the fuel of peace and joy, like oil for fire, because of the strength of his meditative realization.

Lineage

There was only one transmission lineage of the *Profound Dharma of Natural Liberation* up to Gyarawa, Namkha Chokyi Gyatso (Tib. *Rgya ra ba Nam mkha chos kyi rgya mtsho*). After him, the *Profound Dharma of Natural Liberation* spread through many different lineages. The following lineage is based on the transmission that came to the third Dodrupchen Rinpoche (Tib. *rDo grup chen rin po che*) through the Lamas (Tib. *bla mas*) of Mindrol Ling (Tib. *sMin grol gling*) Monastery of Central Tibet and of Dzogchen (Tib. *rDzog chen*) Monastery of Eastern Tibet.

> *Dharmakaya*: the Samantabhadra Consorts
> *Sambhogakaya*: The Buddhas of the Five Classes and Vajradhara
> *Nirmanakaya*: Garab Dorje
>   (Tib. *dGa' rab rdo rje*)
> Srisimha
> Guru Padmasambhava
> Dakini, Yeshe Tshogyal
>   (Tib. *Ye shes mtsho rgyal*)
> Translator, Chog-ro Lu-gysaltsen
>   (Tib. *lCog ro Klu'i rgyal mtshan*, 9th century)
> Great *gter ston*, Karma Lingpa
>   (Tib. *Karma gling pa*, 14th century)
> Thugse, Nyida Choje
>   (Tib. *Thugs sras, Nyi zla chos rje*, 14th century)

Nyida Odzer
 (Tib. *Nyi zla 'od zer*, Suryarasmi)
Gyarawa, Namkha Chokyi Gyatso
 (Tib. *Rgya ra ba, Nam mkha chos kyi rgya mtsho*)
Rigdzin, Sodnam Odzer
 (Tib. *Rig 'dzin, bSod nams 'od zer*)
Drupchen Pynyeshri
 (Tib. *Grub chen, Punyasri*)
Gyalwang, Changchub Lingpa
 (Tib. *rGyal dbang, Byang chub gling pa*, 15th century)
Yongdzin, Sodnam Chokyong
 (Tib. *Yongs 'dzin, bSod nams chos skyong*)
Kunkhyen, Natshog Rangtrol
 (Tib. *Kun mkhyen, sNa tshogs rang grol*, 1494-1560)
Thugse, Kunga Trapa
 (Tib. *Thugs sras, Kun dga' grags pa*)
Sungtul, Tentzin Tragpa
 (Tib. *gSung sprul, bsTan 'dzin grags pa*,1536-1597)
Kunkhyen, Dongag Tendzin
 (Tib. *Kun mkhyen, mDo ngag bstan 'dzin*, 1576-1628)
Rigdzin, Thrinle Lhundrup
 (Tib. *Rig 'dzin, Phrin las lhun grub*, 1611-1662)
Minling Terchen, Gyurmed Dorje
 (Tib. *sMin gling gter chen, 'Gyur med rdo rje*, 646-1714)
Minling Lochen, Dharmashri
 (Tib. *sMin gling lo chen*, Dharmasri, 1654-1717)
First Dzogchen Rinpoche, Padma Rigdzin
 (Tib. *rDzogs chen rin po che, Padma rig 'dzin*, 1625-1697)
First Dzogchen Ponlob, Namkha Odsel
 (Tib. *rDzogs chen dpon slob, Nam mkha 'od gsal*, ?-1726)
Dzogchen Jewon, Padma Kuntrol Namgyal
 (Tib. *rDzogs chen 'ju dbon, Padma kun grol rnam rgyal*,
 1706-1773)
Third Dzogchen Rinpoche, Ngedon Tendzin Zangpo
 (Tib. *rDzogs chen rin po che, Nges don bstan 'dzin bzang po*,
 1759-1792)
Dzogchen Khenchen, Rigdzin Zangpo

(Tib. *rDzogs chen mKhan chen, Rig 'dzin bzang po*)
First Gyarong Namtul, Jigmed Mikyod Dorje
    (Tib. *Rgya rong nam sprul, 'Jigs med mi bskyod rdo rje,*
    1744-?)
Padma Kunzang
    (Tib. *Padma kun bzang*)
Fourth Dzogchen Rinpoche, Jigme Khyentse Wangchug
    (Tib. *rDzogs chen rin po che, 'Jigs med mkhyen brtse
    dbang phyugs,* 1793-?)
Thrinle Namgyal Dorje
    (Tib. *Phrin las rnam rgyal rdo rje*)
Second Gyarong Namtul, Kunzang Thegchog Dorje
    (Tib. *Rgya rong nam sprul, Kun bzang theg mchog rdo rje*)[7]
Third Dodrupchen, Jigme Tenpe Nyima
    (Tib. *rDo grub chen, 'Jigs med bstan pa'i nyi ma,* 1865-1926)

The transmission lineage of the *Profound Dharma of Natural Liberation* that came to Kyabje Dudjom Rinpoche (Tib. *sKyab rje bDud 'joms rin po che*) is the same as that of the Third Dodrupchen Rinpoche up to the lineage of Minling Lochen Dharmadshri. According to my sources, thereafter the transmission lineage of Kyabje Dudjom Rinpoche is as follows:

Minling Lochen Dharmashri
Rinchen Namgyal (Tib. *Rin chen rnam rgyal*)
Padma Tendzin (Tib. *Padma bstan 'dzin*)
Thrinle Namgyal (Tib. *Phrin las rnam rgyal*)
Thrinle Chodron (Tib. *Phrin las chos sgron*)
Jamyang Khyentse Wangpo (Tib. *'Jam dbangs mkhyen brtse
    dbang po*)
Gyurme Ngedon Wangpo (Tib. *'Gyur med nges don dbang po*)
Jigdral Yeshe Dorje (Tib. *'Jigs bral ye shes rdo rje*)

Finally, let me offer my humble gratitude to Master Tam Shek-wing, a direct learned disciple of Kyabje Dudjom Rinpoche, and his dedicated students of the Vajrayana Buddhism Association, for making the essence of the most precious six bardo

---

7   Names up to the Second *Rgya rong nam sprul, Kun bzang theg mchg rdo rje,* are based on rDzogs chen Monastery's lineage given in: *Kar gling zhi khro,* f. 747 (Pub. by Sichuan Mi rigs dpe bskrun khang, China).

teachings from the cycle of the *Profound Dharma of Natural Liberation through the Intention of the Peaceful and Wrathful Ones* available in this English-language commentary and guidebook. May the merits of this great accomplishment cause all mother beings to wake up into the ever secure state of their own naturally liberated vision, as an infant wakes in its mother's lap.

Tulku Thondup, Rinpoche
The Buddhayana Foundation

PART I

Introduction to Fundamental Concepts Related to Natural Liberation

To Undress Our Minds

The Illusory Nature of Cyclic Existence

SINCE THE BEGINNING OF TIME, all of us have lived in an illusory world, engaged in a perpetual cycle of living and dying. Whether we have lived meaningfully or with regrets, our existence continues in a whirlwind of time and space. Many great philosophers and sages have given teachings on how to live meaningfully, in harmony with the natural world. The Daoist classic *Zhuangzi* represents one of the most important works on this subject. *Chiwu* (Embracing Unity), one of the chapters in the *Zhuangzi*, revolves around the axiom of oneness.[1] It says that there is an all-encompassing intrinsic essence permeating the universe. All that exists – you, me, nature and so on – is one, in the essence of *chiwu*. When we attune ourselves with the rhythms of nature, we are immersing ourselves in this innate oneness, the totality of all.

Master Zhuangzi was a real-life example of such an ideal. In his time, he was a highly regarded master, and the Emperor of Chu sent an envoy to invite him to take the seat of premier. When Zhuangzi received the invitation, instead of accepting the offer, he asked the messenger a question: "I heard that in his private shrine room, the Emperor of Chu has an artifact, a relic of a tortoise, three thousand years old. The Emperor cherishes this relic so much that he keeps it in a tiny treasure box on his shrine. Let me ask you this: Do you think the tortoise wanted to die, to have its remains worshipped in secret, or would it have preferred to live, dragging its tail through the muddy old swamp?" The envoy pondered a while and hesitantly answered, "Master, my humble guess is that it would have preferred to live." His indifference to the Emperor's offer revealed, Zhuangzi sent the messenger away: "Please go. That is how I would like to continue my life, wandering through this muddy old swamp." Zhuangzi preferred to live in a simple world of natural order; a world of natural autonomy, where laws, politics and man-made

---

1   The *Zhuangzi* has been translated into English by Burton Watson, among others. See Burton Watson, *The Complete Works of Chuang Tzu* (New York: Columbia University Press, 1968). The chapter on *Chiwu* is found in Chapter 17 of Watson's translation (pp. 175 - 189).

regulations had little meaning. His perfect world was the poetry of natural order and display.

Sadly, for the most part, humankind no longer lives in harmony with the natural world. Rather, we have separated ourselves from nature; instead of seeing ourselves as part of it, see ourselves as masters of it. Our scientific knowledge and technological knowhow have enabled us to create a manmade world that exists in tension with and even domination over the natural world. We too have changed from the ideal of Zhuangzi's time. We are greedy and materialistic, and eager for gratification, the sooner the better. Our remarkable accomplishments in science and technology appear to have improved the quality of human life, but their nature is deceptive. If we investigate, we discover that they are mere smokescreens, blinding us to the true nature of this empirical world of ours, distancing us further from the truth.

Take the example of the invention of the computer. It has transformed the way we gather and store information, do research, entertain ourselves, and even interact with each other. The Internet means ordinary people have access to an incredible volume of information, some of it good, some of it highly question-able. Because of this, we are supposed to live happily in a more communicative environment. But keeping abreast of the latest information or trend has become a challenge that leaves many computer users stressed. In addition to managing information overkill, we must also worry about our computers becoming infected by viruses, worms and spyware. Ironically, some computer users may try to protect personal data when online even while they simultaneously reveal deeply personal information in blogs and on social networking sites; they are more open to total strangers that they are to those who actually know them.

We can also think of how science and technology have given us an array of consumer goods unimaginable a few generations ago. Ever being improved upon, many of these goods are obsolete almost as soon as they hit the market. Confusing need with want, we buy regardless; our consumer society encourages us to hanker after the new and discard the old, and to believe that happiness lies in consuming. This has resulted in a waste of natural and human resources, social and economic dysfunction, and environmental pollution.

We have used our intelligence to create an advanced technological civilization but we have not achieved happiness. We have not created Zhuangzi's utopia of oneness with the natural world. The glory of our civilization is only a facade, yet we are delighted with its appearance. We taste the fruit of suffering, mistakenly believing it to be delectable. Our ignorance can only impel us towards our own demise. I see a pressing need for a remedy for this degenerate age, which was prophesied by the great masters. I remember the profound teachings of my beloved root guru, Dudjom Rinpoche (1904-1987), who incisively pointed out the illusory nature of our world. His words tore away the veil of this grand illusion that we celebrate. Out of his kindness, he revealed the path I should take to become awakened.

Unlike Zhuangzi, who told us to live like tortoises, dragging our tails through a muddy old swamp, Mahayana Buddhism advises us to live in this illusory world as it is, fully and compassionately, yet wakefully. There is no need to escape civilization and flee to the Himalayas in a physical sense. The Mahayana trains us to be in tune with our own awakened nature at all times. We can commit to our illusory world in a wakeful manner and be actively responsible, like players on a stage acting their roles faithfully, passionately and responsibly. We can work and play with clarity and wakefulness, with full understanding that this grand performance of our lives is but a series of appearances arising like an evolving dream. As Dudjom Rinpoche showed me, we can achieve natural liberation in this very life.

This present book is based on the *Guide to the Six Bardos According to the Perfection Stage*[2] from a series of hidden treasure texts (Tib. *gter ma*) known as the *Profound Dharma of Natural Liberation through the Intention of the Peaceful and Wrathful Ones*[3], written by the ancient guru Padmasambhava. The *Guide to the Six Bardos* was discovered in the second half of the 14th century in a cave on Mount Gampodar (Tib. *sgam po gdar*) by the "treasure-discoverer" (Tib. *gter ston*) Karma Lingpa (Tib. *Karma Gling pa*) when he was only 15 years old. He was believed to be the reincarnation of one of the 25 close disciples of Padmasambhava, and possessed extraordinary supernatural cognitive powers.

Bardo means an intermediate or in-between state. The term usually refers to the interim state of existence occurring immediately after death but before rebirth. However, in the teachings of the six bardos, the meaning of bardo is expanded. The six bardos are as follows:

> The bardo of living (Tib. *skye gnas bar do*)
> The bardo of dreams (Tib. *rmi lam bar do*)
> The bardo of meditation (Tib. *fbsam gtan bar do*)

---

2   Tib.: *rDzogs rim bar do drug gi khrid yig*. This cycle is available in English translation: Alan Wallace, trans., *Natural Liberation: Padmasambhava's Teachings on the Six Bardos* (Boston: Wisdom Publications, 1998). Cf. Gyurme Dorje, trans., *First Complete Translation: The Tibetan Book of the Dead* (New York: Penguin Books, 2006).

3   Tib.: *Zab chos zhi khro dgongs pa rang grol*.

The bardo of dying (Tib. *'chi'i kha bar do*)
The bardo of *dharmata* (Tib. *chos nyid bar do*)
The bardo of becoming (Tib. *srid pa bar do*)

These are discussed further in chapter 6 and expanded upon in Part II of this book.

The civilized world of modern humanity and Master Zhuangzi's natural utopia are poles apart. Yet the teachings contained in *Natural Liberation through the Six Bardos* can bridge the gap and awaken us to a new world that is neither an escape from civilization, as his was, nor blind acceptance of it, as ours is. We can be awake and still live in the world. Zhuangzi's utopia is a stage, the curtains of which have never really been opened. In our theatre, however, the curtains have never really been closed. We are so accustomed to dressing in the costumes demanded by our roles that we have forgotten the freedom gained from being undressed. In the theatrical hologram that we call reality, we are given an alternative path that offers liberation, a path that can train us to play at ease on the stage that is samsara. We can learn to be mindful to let our curtains close, and let our minds undress at the same time. In this special theatre of our mind, we are continually performing our repertoire while the curtain is continually closing. And at every moment, here and now, our mind is continually undressing, resting completely in its naked awareness. We have entered the inconceivable world of Dharma.

Chapter 2

Liberating our Minds from the Cycle of Living and Dying

It has been said that people in the west live in a death-denying culture, yet deny as we might, we know in our hearts that we cannot live forever. Death always awaits us, each moment of our life taking us closer to the moment of our death. Because an understanding of death is so fundamental to Buddhist spiritual practice, in the teachings on the six bardos, the very first teaching is a meditation on death. By meditating on death, we first come to understand it, and then, as we progress in our meditation practice, we liberate ourselves from the endless cycle of birth, death and rebirth.

Human existence is bounded by the dimensions of space and time. We see our lives in terms of where and when. This spatio-temporal preoccupation means we see birth as the beginning of life and death as its end. When we take on a form of existence in a certain space and time, we are said to be living; when we pass from it, we are said to be dead. However, in truth, what we call death in the spatio-temporal realm where we now find ourselves is also birth in another; through the practice of meditation, we learn to see that there is no space, no time, no birth and no death. When we achieve liberation, we understand space and time as concepts that frame our conventional world, and living and dying as mere phenomena that arise and fall away within it.

Even in our everyday life, lived within its finite frame of space and time, we recognize the gross impermanence that is birth becoming death. When we look at the stages of life, from infancy through childhood, adolescence, adulthood, middle age, to old age, we can see gross impermanence at work. All phenomena, natural or man-made, manifest gross impermanence. Acorns become oak trees, oak trees die and return to the soil from which they arose; new buildings become derelict and crumble to dust. If we look more closely, we understand that impermanence is pervasive; with every single phenomenon, at every single moment, there is a coincidental process of beginning and ceasing. For example, the moment a flower blossoms, the state of that flower as "not yet blossomed" ceases. If the "not yet blossomed" state does not cease, then the fully opened blossom cannot come to be. Similarly, in metabolic processes, the generation of new cells occurs simultaneously with the degeneration of old cells. Arising and ceasing are two aspects of a single process. This is subtle impermanence. The Buddha taught that everything that is produced (in other words, that comes into being), also passes away. Impermanence is as true for the cosmos as it is for a single cell.

An understanding of impermanence can help dissolve our rigid notion of the past, present and future as being composed of distinct moments of life demarcated by birth at the beginning and death at the end. Instead, we can experience a continuum of simultaneous becoming and ceasing has neither beginning nor end. For example, we typically see fossils or other prehistoric or historic remains as having existed entirely separately from ourselves. With an understanding of impermanence, however, we see that their becoming and ceasing to be is at one with our own becoming and ceasing. Looking at phenomena in this way is not mental trickery intended to deceive, but rather an important practice that helps us let go of conventional ideas about living and dying.

Permanence is an unchanging phenomenon. However, permanence is not a characteristic of the phenomena of our world. Everything in our world is impermanent, arising according to causes and conditions and then ceasing to be, subject to the cycle of living and dying. Do we understand this at a deep level? So much of human endeavour is spent trying to prevent change, to keep things the way we think they should be. Emperors in ancient times exerted extraordinary effort to build empires that would endure for generations; they used their wealth and power to create monuments to themselves so that their fame would last forever. The Alchemists of old, who wanted to transmute base metals into gold, also hoped to find the secret of eternal life. Alchemy was first developed in Egypt and quickly spread to China. In China, the Daoist school of Alchemy, known as Elixir, thrived. These scholars focused on developing an elixir for preserving youth and increasing longevity, and even claimed to have developed a formula to ensure immortality. Although they called themselves Daoists, their pursuit of everlasting life clearly departed from Laozi's teachings of *wuwei* or "non-action" and Zhuangzi's philosophy of *chiwu* or "embracing unity," which together are the cornerstones of philosophical Daoism. Our own time is characterized by a somewhat similar quest for eternal youth and beauty in the form of scientific breakthroughs that would slow down or even reverse the ageing process. But in truth, permanence is a chimera.

How then should we reflect upon impermanence so as to deepen our understanding of it? We could perhaps begin by examining our attachment to permanence by observing some common examples in our daily lives. For instance, when we meet our first love, we want the infatuation to last forever. Similarly, when we are enjoying prosperity and worldly success, we hope that our fortunate situation will continue uninterrupted. Further, despite all the evidence to the contrary, many of us think and act as if we will live forever.

We have to be careful with our understanding of impermanence and not let it degenerate into nihilism, a world view tainted with pessimism, indifference and disrespect. Just because everything passes does not mean that we should not care. When a baby is born, it is not helpful to go to the extreme and think pessimistically that the infant is falling into the hands of the Lord of Death. Similarly, when we have just witnessed the first shoots of a flower, it is counter-productive to be overwhelmed by the thought of a withered flower. Put into practice, nihilism can result in the extremes of hedonism or totalitarianism. The former, hedonism, was preached in India by Charvaka, who urged people to live their lives to the full, seeking pleasure and gratification in the here and now. The latter, totalitarianism, developed from racist ideology, and is characterized by an egocentric extremism that is disrespectful of the value of life.

When we transcend the constraints built by space and time, and allow our minds to observe the phenomena of arising, abiding, changing and ceasing in a non-conceptual context, we can easily find equilibrium free of the extremes of permanence and nihilism. The equilibrium free of these two extremes is called "not perpetuating, not annihilating."

When a phenomenon ceases to exist, its effects may still continue. For this reason, we cannot say in absolute terms that it has completely died. We can only say that it is impermanent. A phenomenon of which a principal characteristic is that it and its effects change every moment is not permanent either. We might say it is unendingly impermanent, with its effects reverberating endlessly like a butterfly's wings in Chaos Theory. A butterfly flapping its wings beside the River Nile may cause a series of weather changes, which in turn could cause a devastating tornado in the Amazon Rainforest. Due to amplification of each related effect, the system over time becomes chaotic and unpredictable.

The world in which we live is, in fact, such a chaotic world. If we investigate our world at a microscopic level, the theories of light as being composed of continuous waves and of matter as being composed of discrete particles lose some of their validity. After close observation of a spectrum of light, scientists discovered that it is composed of a continuous display of discrete lines of colour, rather than a continuous wave. Light as a phenomenon is thus discrete and continuous, analogous to phenomena described as "not perpetuating, not annihilating." Contrary to our ordinary perception of energy as insubstantial and matter as solid, Quantum Theory describes both energy and matter as both waves and particles. Energy exhibiting wavelike behaviour can be described in terms of particles, while matter that seems solid can be described in the context of waves. The physical and non-physical modes of existence that we perceive as separate switch back and forth from moment to moment. Our senses are both discretely and continuously experiencing such dimensions of time and space. This experience is what we call not perpetuating, not annihilating.

When we dissolve the rigidity of our perception of time and space, and observe phenomena from a higher perspective as if we have entered the unseen dimension described by modern physicists, we will undergo a brand new experience of things. We may notice a world a billion times more chaotic. Yet, in this chaos, a natural rhythm of change exists – the rhythm that is not perpetuating, not annihilating. If we perceive all phenomena as having this intrinsic rhythm, we will discover natural liberation from within. Observing the phenomena as unproduced and unending, not perpetuating and not annihilating, is essential to the practice of the six bardos. This practice liberates our minds from the interlocking chains of constraints, allowing us to attain true liberation. A mind that sees beyond the constraints of time and space is naturally liberating. We become freed from egocentricity and selfishness and at one with the eternal rhythm of becoming and ceasing.

CHAPTER 3

Experiencing the Cycle of Living and Dying in One Meditation Session

I F WE WANT TO MAKE PROGRESS in the Dharma practice of *The Six Bardos of Living and Dying*, we need to further our understanding of rebirth and the various forms of existence in the six realms. In everyday discourse, the Buddhist concept of rebirth is sometimes conflated with the Hindu concept of reincarnation, but in fact the two concepts are somewhat different. In Buddhism, it is consciousness that travels from life to life; in Hinduism, it is a fixed self. By whatever name we call it, reincarnation or rebirth, and however we define it, the subject is a controversial one in today's world. Does the phenomenon of reincarnation really exist? Do the six realms of existence really exist? Because these tenets of faith cannot be proven beyond doubt, many people are skeptical about their validity.

Certainly, without convincing scientific evidence, the existence of reincarnation is difficult for many to people to accept; for this reason, any careful research into reincarnation by an established academic immediately catches our attention. In his book *Twenty Cases Suggestive of Reincarnation*[1], Ian Stevenson presents 20 cases of reincarnation, some vividly rich in detail. Many of the places and events remembered are traceable; the author states that some cases are "fully authenticated by many witnesses." His studies provide considerable evidence that there are people who can recall their past lives. Stevenson's book is a good reference for those seeking an affirmative answer to the question of reincarnation.

However, while many schools of Buddhism welcome scientific proof of reincarnation, such proof is not crucial to the Dharma practice of *The Six Bardos of Living and Dying*. This Dharma practice allows practitioners to gain realization through daily observation and contemplation of rebirth and the six realms of existence as they appear in everyday human life. Even if scientists were to prove that reincarnation or rebirth is so much spiritual hocus pocus, it would not affect

---

[1]   Ian Stevenson, *Twenty Cases Suggestive of Reincarnation* (Charlottesville: University Press of Virginia, 1974).

the power of this Dharma practice because the Dharma is beyond existence and nonexistence, beyond reality and illusion. As previously discussed, the Dharma teaches that all phenomena are mere appearances, like illusions or dreams. Our living and dying are merely fleeting moments of this illusory vision. If reincarnation were to be proven beyond a doubt, we would only have succeeded in confirming a dream within a dream. On the other hand, if reincarnation were ever convincingly refuted, only an illusion would have been disproven.

The Six Realms

How can we establish the validity of the concepts of rebirth and the six realms? Why is it necessary to do so? To make our Dharma practice truly meaningful, we need to develop a genuine realization of renunciation. As it is used in Buddhism, renunciation refers specifically to the state of mind that wants to be freed from the illusion of cyclic existence or samsara, which has the nature of suffering. Since beginning-less time, we have taken rebirth after rebirth in samsara. Sometimes we have taken a higher rebirth, sometimes a lower, but every rebirth has had its share of suffering. Except in the hell realms, where suffering is unmitigated, we also have a share of pleasure. Whichever form we take, we spend our lifetime trying to find pleasure and avoid pain. There can be no lasting peace of mind until we free ourselves from illusion.

Buddhist texts often contain cosmological references that describe the six realms according to the characteristics of the three *kleshas* (Skt. *klesha*) or poisons, being the three principal negative emotions – greed or desire, hatred and self-grasping. The six realms, from lowest to highest, are the hell realm, the realm of the hungry ghosts, the animal realm, the human realm, the demi-god realm and the god realm.

The hell realm, the lowest of the lower realms, is a world of hatred and vengeance. Hell beings are trapped in a state of intense torment, experiencing bone-crushing agony in every moment of their existence. Some are burnt in an environment baked by unceasing, raging fire. Others must endlessly endure the pain of having their skins cracked open and their bodies shattered into pieces by the biting cold. There are forests in this realm, but they are made of sword-leaf trees with razor-sharp edges, ready to dismember the bones and limbs of its inhabitants. From these chilling descriptions we can infer the depth of the hatred inherent to the hell realm.

The realm of the hungry ghosts is the second of the lower realms. In Buddhist texts, hungry ghosts are vividly described as extraordinarily greedy. Their throats are so narrow, it is painful for them to eat more than a small bite. Consequently, they are constantly hungry; they spend their lives looking for food. They cannot bear to lose a single opportunity to seize the food of others, and, of course, they never share with others.

The third of the lower realms is the animal realm, and is discernible to our senses. The ignorance existing there is self-evident. Animals live in a state of constant fear and insecurity. Predator and prey alike spend their lives searching for food and shelter. These creatures react instinctively under the grasping of their "I," and can be no more than predator or prey. Only the fittest survive.

The human realm is the lowest of the three higher realms, and is characterized by self-grasping ignorance. Our unrelenting grasping of our I becomes the backdrop to all our self-cherishing acts. This I can sometimes expand to include an entire country or even the whole human race. In contrast, it can shrink to embrace only the self. All matters outside its boundary, whether people or events, are in perpetual conflict with the I. The innate discord between the I and others will always be a source of endless clashes. However harmonious the relationship between I and others may appear, intrinsic dissonance will not allow harmony to last. Self-grasping ignorance is the source of all suffering.

The remaining two higher realms are the demi-god realm and the god realm. They are uneasy neighbours. According to the texts, the gods in the higher realms are greedy and full of desire. From the moment they are born, they live lives of pleasure and indulgence, and yet they are not satisfied. Throughout their lives, they are cosseted by the sweet fragrance of garlands, sumptuous arrays of delectable foods, rapturous music and the love of beautiful goddesses. Even so, they seek the company of the demigoddesses, thus causing terrible jealousy amongst the demigods. Again according to the texts, the demigods are very ugly, but the demigoddesses are extremely attractive and very desirable. The demigoddesses are often lured away by the gods. Worse, there is a tall, wish-fulfilling tree, with its trunk and roots in the demigod realm, but its flowers and fruits in the god realm. The demigods have the duty of watering the tree but no chance to taste its fruits. The gods can pick the fruits at their leisure; when they cut these fruits open, all their wishes are granted. How can the demigods not be jealous?

To develop renunciation, it is not necessary to have scientific evidence of reincarnation or rebirth or of the six realms. We can understand the six realms as being apt descriptions of the world in which we live. In fact, the six realms can be observed and experienced in our everyday lives, in the here and now. For example, people living in violent conditions where they under constant threat exist in a kind of hell realm. Similarly, people who want, want, want but who are never satisfied are like hungry ghosts. The animal and human realms are quite apparent to us; we have no need of proof. Within the human realm, we can see humans who, blessed with good fortune, live like demi-gods or gods. According to the descriptions of the demi-god realm, the sentient beings there live almost as well as gods, but not quite; their pleasures, comforts, and status are less; they are like the prosperous middle class as opposed to the super rich. The gods are like the celebrities of samsara, beautiful and privileged, living lives of extraordinary pleasure and indulgence. However, even they do not have complete happiness, troubled as they are by memories of their former lives and premonitions of their future lower rebirths. For most of their lives, the gods are happily oblivious to the suffering of the lower realms. They only become aware of it when they are about to take a lower rebirth themselves.

Even though we humans can see suffering all around us, we still remain unconvinced of the true nature of samsara. We should want to free ourselves, but all too often we do not. Instead, we live in hope that things will get better. Not only have we failed to develop a genuine heart of renunciation; but our attachment to samsara is such that we dread the moment of death when we must bid this life goodbye. However, if we could see samsara for what it is, our renunciation would become definite and immediate. The way to do this is through meditation.

Meditation Practice (1)

We begin by meditating on the countless cycles of living, dying and rebirth as if we have actually experienced them. In truth, no matter how mundane our lives seem, we have actually passed through many such cycles. For example, when a baby grows from infancy into childhood, she or he has gone through a cycle of living, dying and rebirth. The same is true for other stages of human life. When childhood becomes adolescence, adolescence adulthood or adulthood senescence, a cycle of living, dying and rebirth takes place. Periods of major change or upheaval in our lives where we emerge different than we were before are also cycles of living, dying and rebirth. Through carefully reviewing the stages of our own lives, and reflecting on the many ups and downs we have experienced, we can come to accept the validity of the concepts of rebirth and the six realms and from that acceptance, a realization of renunciation will follow quickly.

Meditation Practice (2)

We can also meditate and reflect upon the examples of greed, hatred and ignorance in the six realms. Are they not the same as we experience in our present lives as we navigate its ups and downs? Every moment of our existence is tainted by the three poisons. Meditating on the six realms allows us to recognize the imprints of the root delusions in our own minds, from which the external phenomena of our lives are composed.

When contemplating examples of greed or desire, hatred and ignorance, we should not make the mistake of thinking that any of these three poisons can have a positive aspect. To do so would be wrong-headed. For example, if someone amasses a fortune through greed and then donates some of that fortune to a worthy cause, the greed is not magically transformed into generosity. Greed and generosity are two different states of mind, the first negative and the second positive. Similarly, desire and love are not two sides of the same coin; rather, they are two entirely different states of mind. A desirous mind never sees the object of its desire clearly, and is driven by self-centredness. It says "If I possess this I will be happy." Our notion of romantic love is in fact a form of desire. A mind of love, on the other hand, puts others before itself, and wants them to be happy; love is a positive state of mind. Hatred, like desire, is always a negative mind; there is no such thing as a positive manifestation of hatred. While most interpersonal and intergroup conflict may arise out of hatred, not all of it does; it may sometimes arise out of a mind of love, as in a valiant struggle against tyranny and oppression. Finally, the third root delusion, self-grasping ignorance, cannot ever have a positive side. When we speak of ignorance with respect to the three poisons, we mean our failure to understand the true nature of reality and our grasping at ourselves and other phenomena as existing inherently.

When we meditate upon the six realms, we gain experience of the cycles of living and dying. Indeed, we can go through several cycles of living and dying in one meditation session. In this way, through accepting the concept of rebirth and the six realms, we gain control over our minds and liberate ourselves from illusory cyclic existence.

We can take our meditation further by transforming the illusory phenomena of the six realms of samsara into halos of light, which we then immerse in the clear, cloudless sky, allowing them to dissolve into the vast horizon. We let them completely vanish, without a trace, leaving behind a vast expanse of radiant, luminous iridescence. In this moment, here and now, we have cycled through samsara and entered a kind of nirvana. We relinquish our grasp and recognize our rebirth into a new state of awareness – the awareness of the newly born, free from all material elaborations. We have returned to our original heart of delight, the source of peace, harmony and wisdom.

CHAPTER 4

Understanding the Concept of Naturally Arisen Phenomena

IT IS INTEGRAL TO THE PRACTICE of the Nyingma School that we understand the concept of naturally arisen phenomena (Tib. *rang snang*). Because all phenomena are naturally arisen, it follows that natural liberation (Tib. *rang grol*) is achievable.

Naturally Arisen Phenomena

What is the meaning of naturally arisen? Naturally arisen phenomena can be perceived and experienced as two kinds: samsaric and nirvanic. In samsara, naturally arisen phenomena are in a state of constraint, bound and conditioned. These phenomena adapt to the conditions of existence of the particular realm in which they appear. For example, when a sentient being in a realm of three-dimensional space and one-directional time is perceived in a realm of N-dimensional space and M-directional time, her or his appearance manifests in accordance with that of N-dimensional space and M-directional time. We are already simultaneously appearing in all realms, which interpenetrate each other. It is not that we actually move from one realm to another, but rather that we are perceived with a different set of parameters, depending on the realm in which we are perceived. Simply put, our appearance is relative to the realm in which we appear.

Yet, despite naturally arisen phenomena being bound and conditioned, natural liberation occurs effortlessly by itself, independent of the compulsion of others, much like a cobra that uncoils itself in its basket. The terms naturally arisen and natural liberation are sometimes translated into English as self-arisen and self-liberation. Constrained by our consciousness though we may be, we are the ones who release ourselves from our coiled state. Nagarjuna explained naturally arisen phenomena in the context of dependent relationships. All the manifestations of our lives and the empirical world around us are adventitious phenomena.

Their arising depends entirely on the ripening of causes and conditions – in other words, karma. Causes can be regarded as subjective elements, while conditions can be deemed objective environmental factors. Phenomena that arise naturally from karma are said to be naturally arisen. In samsara, all phenomena are bound by the laws of karma, the laws of cause and effect. Karma resides in our mental continuum like seeds kept in a granary, ready to ripen when the necessary conditions are present. No one except ourselves can create our karma for us; no one else can change it. For this reason, when we discuss naturally arisen in samsara, we can speak in the context of self-arisen.

There is a story about the goddess of garlands that illustrates the meaning of naturally arisen in the context of self-arisen. A king invited Buddha Shakyamuni to his palace to give teachings. The queen, princes, princesses and their maids were among the listeners. One princess was so stirred by Buddha Shakyamuni's words that she quietly asked her maid to fetch her most precious garland of pearls to offer to Buddha Shakyamuni. Her maid was reluctant to go because she didn't want to miss the blessings of the teachings. But suddenly the Buddha's lessons on impermanence flashed through her mind. She considered, "All phenomena are impermanent. If I were to die in the next moment, I would not have the opportunity to offer a gift to Buddha Shakyamuni. No matter what blessings I receive from listening to his teachings, it would not offset my not making the precious offering to him." Without further delay, she left to fetch the garland of pearls. On her way back, dark storm clouds suddenly rose over the horizon. The wind blew, lightening flashed, thunder crashed and the rain came down in sheets. A bolt of lightning struck the maid, killing her instantly. The king and his family carefully carried the maid's body inside, hoping that Buddha Shakyamuni would bring her back to life. However, instead of doing this, the Buddha bestowed his blessings on the maid by teaching about karma. Her being struck by lightning was caused by negative karma created in a previous life. But she must have also created some very positive karma, for, although only a servant, she listened to and understood teachings from the Buddha himself. Because of this, prior to her death, she attained a realization of impermanence. When she acted upon it to make an offering to the Buddha, she created even more positive karma for her future lives. This story reveals the intricacies of meaning to naturally arisen in the context of self-arisen. The maid's death was naturally arisen upon the ripening of a cause created in her previous lives. However, her self-arising virtuous intent in making the offering established the act as virtuous, thus creating positive karma for her future lives. If she had acted without any virtuous intent, the whole story would have ended differently. Her act would not have accumulated any merit worthy of praise by the Buddha.

Karma is created by our mental and physical actions, over which we always have a choice. We can choose to act, or choose not to act. Rather than rigidly pre-determining our actions and our lives, karma abounds with possibilities because we always have a choice. Whichever choice we make affects what arises in the future; all that arises for us stems from the karma we have created. The realm into which we are born, and our life experiences within in that realm are the effects of causes we have created by our actions in previous lives. For example, we may have created the cause to be born human, but in an environment where life is a constant struggle. Or, more positively, we may have created the cause to be born into a world where the Dharma thrives. All is but the manifestation of karma. Generally speaking, our choices imprison us further in the web of our karma, and we continue to experience the endlessly repeating pattern of living and dying. However, we could choose liberation instead. All self-arisen phenomena can be, and have to be, self-liberated. If we look to others to liberate us, we have fallen into the fallacy of believing that everything is predetermined and that free will is therefore impossible. In samsara, all effects arise naturally from self-created causes; thus, when we talk about naturally arisen phenomena, we can also describe them as self-arisen.

As stated earlier, unlike phenomena in samsara, naturally arisen phenomena in nirvana are unconditioned and unbound. There is neither cobra nor coil to unwind. In nirvana, phenomena are naturally arisen in essence, and exist beyond the samsaric concept of self. When speaking about nirvana, we do not normally use the terms self-arisen and self-liberation. In the next section, we will discuss "naturally arisen" phenomena in nirvana. To begin, I will introduce the concept of primordial ground (Tib. *gdod ma'i gzhi*) from which the phenomena of samsara and nirvana naturally arise.

Primordial Ground

The concept of primordial ground has not been touched upon in our previous discussion of naturally arisen phenomena of samsara because the arising of samsaric phenomena is dependent upon the dimensions of time and space, and adapts to particular conditions. As stated above, all phenomena that arise in our samsaric realm are bound and conditioned by three-dimensional space and one-directional time. However, nirvana is beyond time and space. If we attempt to explain nirvana in the context of our conditioned empirical world, we could easily be misled and misinterpret it as a three-dimensional space where past, present and future exist. For this reason, it is essential that the new concept of primordial ground be explained before any meaningful explanation of naturally arisen phenomena in nirvana is possible.

To attain a more comprehensive description of primordial ground, we need to introduce some new terminology. We must be aware, however, that this terminology is but human language, itself a product of our limitations. Because space and time are the backdrops to our awareness, against which we name our world, all that we can rationalize – that is, put into words – has inherent limits. In truth, nirvana is ultimately inconceivable and beyond words.

The essence of primordial ground is empty. This concept is the principal teaching of the Buddha: Buddhism teaches that all phenomena lack inherent existence. To describe any phenomenon, whether animate or inanimate, as inherently existing is to depart from the Buddha's teaching of the three marks of existence in samsara: impermanence (Skt. *anicca*), not-self (Skt. *anatman*) and suffering (Skt. *dukkha*).

The nature of primordial ground-itself is the *Dharmakaya* of primordial ground, also known as "before *Dharmakaya*," or *tathagatagarbha*. Its nature is unchanging; it has been compared to a vast, empty sky. Although the *Dharmakaya* of primordial ground can be temporarily obscured, much a clear sky may become overcast, its intrinsically empty nature is not affected. The expression of primordial ground is luminosity. In a wider context, technically, it should be referred to as a natural cognizant. This natural cognizant is complete in itself; it is not created by causes and its ever-luminous nature will not cease due to defilements or impurities. We can compare such luminosity to the reflective quality of a mirror. Even when the mirror is covered with a fine film of dust, its innate reflective nature is not altered. This luminosity is referred to as the *Sambhogakaya*, or Enjoyment body, of primordial ground.

Primordial ground has the faculty to encompass all that naturally arises. It includes all naturally arisen phenomena, and pervades all realms of space and time, including samsara and nirvana. It adapts to different dimensions of space and time, arising as respectively adapted displays. Because its naturally adapts to different realms, it not only pervades all time and space but also nirvana. In the human realm of three-dimensional space and one-directional time, the display of luminosity arises spontaneously. We term its inherent naked responsiveness as spontaneous. Like a mirror, it naturally reflects everything without discrimination; its all-encompassing quality does not distinguish between male and female, rich and poor, beautiful and homely. This all-encompassing faculty is the *Nirmanakaya* of primordial ground.

The expression of primordial ground arises spontaneously in and responds nakedly to all dimensions. The all-pervasive, naturally arisen phenomena in samsara and nirvana are the boundless vitalities of the *Dharmadhatu* or realm of Reality. In Buddhist terms, we can describe them as the qualities of the Buddhas. The possibilities pervading all dimensions represent the boundless compassion of the Buddhas.

Such teaching on the three aspects explains the essential meanings of primordial ground according to its nature or essence, expression and inherent capability. We can use a very simple yet modern example to further illustrate this concept. Imagine a vast, clear sky filled with the waves of broadcast frequencies of different television stations. A television set can receive these signals and display them as different television programs. In this example, the boundless sky is comparable to the nature of primordial ground (*Dharmakaya*). The different broadcasting signals filling the sky are analogous to the expression of primordial ground (*Sambhogakaya*), which has the potential for a multitude of displays. The naturally arisen displays on the television screen are akin to the faculty of primordial ground compassionately emanating in the form of fully enlightened beings (*Nirmanakaya*). This example, although not correct in the absolute sense, can help us understand the concept. When we talk about phenomena in nirvana, we describe them as naturally arisen, not self-arisen. Like the example of the sun, from which light and energy radiate indiscriminately, the all-encompassing expressive qualities of primordial ground are naturally abundant with teeming possibilities pervading all dimensions.

This concludes our explanation of the concept of primordial ground. In summary, emptiness has special meaning according to its essence, expression and inherent capability. From this analysis, we have paralleled the Nyingma School's teachings of the three aspects of primordial ground:

> Its essence is primordially pure (nature);
> Its luminous nature is expressed spontaneously as
>   naturally arisen display (expression);
> Its all-encompassing compassion pervades all (faculty).

We need to remember that naturally arisen phenomena are both uncontrived and beyond conceptual fabrication. Like the reflection of the moon on the surface of a calm lagoon, the reflection involves neither initiative nor response. The rising of the moon's reflection is not caused by the lagoon's intention to reflect, nor is it the moon's intention to be reflected. Gaining direct experience through meditation is the best way to understand naturally arisen phenomena. Because of its uncontrived nature, excessive analysis may not divulge its essential meanings. If we want to practice according to the teaching of the three aspects, we must be in unison with primordial ground. We have to begin the practice of experiencing naturally aris- ing. If we only understand the nature of phenomena and not their all-pervasive, naturally arisen qualities, we have not yet gained the key to unlock the path to liberation. When we understand naturally arisen phenomena, we will easily recog- nize that our minds are actually shackled by our own chains, like snakes that loop themselves in coils. Looking at the following two processes, we can examine in greater detail how we imprison ourselves.

The Emptiness of All Phenomena

From the moment we are born into this world, we immediately grasp onto our egocentric selves as I, and look upon the world as revolving around us. From this firmly established position, we regard all phenomena other than our I as external to us. We segregate our I from others by distinguishing between "mine" and "theirs." These discriminations establish I as the subject or viewer, and all other phenomena as objects or the viewed. From this subject-object duality, we commence the labelling process. Every name is embedded within our innate sense of reasoning. We have created countless labels, from "mother," "son," "waterfalls" and "rainbows" to "world wide web" and "Internet." Buddhists do not reject the usefulness of the function of these names and concepts. These names and concepts have practical functions. We depend on them to organize our everyday world, to manipulate it, to accumulate and share knowledge, and to communi- cate to others. Rather, Buddhists refute the inherent existence of labelled objects derived from subject-object duality. If an object exists inherently, it means that its nature is not adventitiously created; it is unchanging and exists independently of others. However, all phenomena lack inherent existence. Thus, Buddhists say all phenomena are empty.

The best analogy is to compare our world of phenomena to a television pro- gram. In this show, each actor is bound by her or his own subject-object duality and that of the character being played. They are playing with labels and concepts, exchanging one set for another. In the show, all the actors and actresses are totally drawn in, and perform their roles as if they were real, yet when they step out of the television studio, they immediately realize that everything inside was merely an illusion. They may not realize that everything outside is also an illusion, an effect of their karma. If we remain attached to the roles we play, our minds will continue to be confined. When we realize that we are actors, our karma is the script we ourselves have written, and reality is our studio, our minds will be liberated instantly. This is what is meant by naturally arisen and naturally liberated.

To attain a naturally liberated state, we must truly understand the conditions from which we are liberating ourselves, being subject-object duality and labels and concepts. Otherwise, we will continue to make choices that will further ensnare us in samsara. For example, if we make a charitable donation with the intention of attracting admiration, our action will only feed our self-cherishing ego, further segregating our I from others. There will be no progress in terms of liberation. Indeed, we may be sinking further into the embrace of subject-object duality. Buddhist masters emphasize the importance of remembering the "emptiness of the three wheels" when making donations. We need to understand that the natures of the donor, the recipient and the charity are all empty. When we donate with the mindfulness of the emptiness of the three wheels we are, on one hand, like an actor on television performing the act of donation, and, on the other hand, like a viewer who can see that the act is only an episode of a television program, and empty of inherent existence. When we bear in mind the emptiness of the three wheels, we are able to influence the mind-itself. Many spiritual teachings focus on influencing our emotions, our gross discursive mind. On the other hand, Buddhist training targets more subtle levels of mind, and trenchantly addresses the very heart of our samsaric problems. Our understanding of natural liberation and naturally arisen phenomena is the key to natural liberation.

If we want to know whether we are making progress on the path of liberation, we must examine our mind. Is it resting nakedly at ease? Having a calm appearance is not a criterion; neither is calming our discursive thoughts or pacifying our emotions so we can rest comfortably on our sofa. Rather, natural liberation means uncoiling ourselves, taking ourselves back to our original liberated state, a state teeming with inconceivable dynamism and possibilities.

CHAPTER 5

Natural Liberation and *Tathagatagarbha*

Natural Liberation through Recognizing the Nucleus of Enlightenment

SOME PEOPLE THINK THAT DEATH BRINGS PEACE: the end to pain and suffering. They are mistaken. According to the teachings of rebirth and the six realms, death is no more than a door to our next life, which will bring us more of the same karmic mix. When we speak of a dead person "being at peace" of putting an animal "out of its misery," or of "being better off dead," we are being deluded. If our life is in danger, we should try to save ourselves; and we should never forfeit our precious human life out of despair. Death does not bring cessation of suffering. When we die, we simply change our form to that of a bardo being and prepare to take yet another rebirth in one of the six realms of samsara. Our karma follows us like a shadow. After death, everything is the same; death changes only our naturally arising appearance. Naturally arising means that all phenomena are mere appearances arising from our mind. Nothing exists inherently beyond our mind. Everything we experience as solidly real is illusory, lacking any inherent existence and empty in nature. This is the true nature of all phenomena.

What is Natural Liberation?

In order to understand the deep meaning of natural liberation, we first need to understand some technical terms. First of all, we need to know what is meant by the true nature of all phenomena. One of the most important works in Chan Buddhism, the preface to *The Origin of Chan* by Guifeng Zongmi (780-841), which was written during the Tang dynasty, explains that:

> The true nature of all phenomena,
> Is not only the foundation of Chan,
> But also the origin of all Dharma,
> Thus it is named *dharmata*;

It is also the source of delusions of all sentient beings,
Thus it is named *tathagatagarbha-alayavijnana*;
And also the essence of the boundless merits of all Buddhas,
Thus it is named *Buddha nature*;
And also the basis of quintessential deeds of the Bodhisattvas,
Thus it is named *grounds*.

From the perspective of the world of phenomena, the true nature of all phenomena is *dharmata* or reality-itself. It is the origin from which all the phenomena of *Dharmakaya* arise. True nature is like a mirror and the phenomena of *Dharmakaya* are like the reflections on its surface. We are often trapped in our own mistaken viewpoints, however, and tenaciously hold onto the myriad reflections in the mirror as being solidly real. We sometimes even reify these illusions and insist they are really objective. Our grasping minds prevent us from seeing beyond the veils of our own delusions. To liberate ourselves is to free us from our obstructions.

From the perspective of sentient beings, the true nature is *tathagatagarbha-alayavijnana*. *Tathagata* refers to the awakened one, and *garbha* means embryo, source, the unborn, nature or origin. *Tathagatagarbha* refers, in general terms, to the awakening mind that is always present, but that is obscured by our delusions. It is Buddha nature. *Alayavijnana* means storehouse consciousness, which is the basis of our mind in its deluded state. These specialized terms are referenced in the *Lankavatara Sutra*.

When sentient beings do not recognize the true nature of all phenomena, and mistakenly grip onto mirrored reflections as solidly existing, Buddhists describe it as unawareness or deluded mind. While we are chained to our own delusions, our consciousness (in Buddhist terms, *alayavijnana*) takes authorship of our experience, thoughts and actions, leaving us blindly succumbing to our fate, oblivious to our options. Upon awakening, we realize that all phenomena are mere displays, like doves or rabbits conjured up in a magic show. The awakened state has a special name, *tathagatagarbha*. Veiled by our delusions, *tathagatagarbha* is in the state of our storehouse consciousness, *alayavijnana*. Through wisdom, we are able to pierce the veil of illusions and recognize our true nature within: *tathagatagarbha*. From the human perspective, *tathagatagarbha-alayavijnana* is the source of the delusions of all sentient beings. Thus, the way to natural liberation is to return to the state of *tathagatagarbha*.

The boundless merits of the Buddhas are spontaneous displays of the true nature, of *tathagatagarbha*. The Nyingma lineage often uses the sun as an analogy.

The true nature is analogous to the sun's nature, while the Buddhas' virtues are analogous to the sun's rays. The inseparability of Buddhas and Buddhas' virtues are analogous to that of the sun and its all-pervading sunlight. Where there is a sun, its energy will naturally suffuse all space without discrimination. These spontaneous displays are the nature of the sun. Likewise, the spontaneously arising merits of the Buddhas are Buddha nature. Buddha nature is the true nature.

Since Bodhisattvas are not fully enlightened beings, they need to practice continuously to attain ultimate realization. They must progress through different levels of practice to attain the ultimate realization of the primordially pure, quintessential state of mind. The qualities of exalted awareness at different levels of attainment are called grounds (Skt. *bhumi*). Bodhisattvas advance from the first to the tenth ground by perfecting their practices. Thus from the perspective of the Bodhisattvas, the grounds are the true nature.

If we are under the direction of our *alayavijnana*, then how can we calm our restless discursive mind thoughts and return to our primordially pure *tathagatagarbha* within?

Master Zongmi further commented:

> Practitioners of the three vehicles, please listen.
> The only path to attain enlightenment is the practice of Chan.
> We cannot deviate from this path,
> As there is no other path.
> For those who wish to take rebirth in the pure land
>   through chanting the name of Amitabha,
> It is essential for them to follow the sixteen practices of Chan
>   visualization.
> Chant in the meditative state of the *Samaya*
> Absorb in the meditative state of *Pratyutpanna-Samadhi*.

In these verses, Chan refers to cultivation of the mind. Master Zongmi reiterated the importance of training the mind. He advised followers of doctrines of the Pure Land, who focus largely on chanting, to include at least the sixteen visualization practices as described in the *Sutra of Contemplation on Buddha Amitayus*. The concept of natural liberation can thus be explained as follows...

We imprison ourselves under the chains of our own *alayavijnana*. Unable to resist its powerful, delusive attraction, we fail to recognize that all phenomena are but the merits of the Buddhas, and we view the illusory appearances as solidly real. To combat this root delusion, we need to train our minds through Dharma practice. We must progress through different grounds until we realize our primordially pure *tathagatagarbha*. The moment we realize *tathagatagarbha* is the moment we attain natural liberation. It is called natural liberation because we are naturally liberated through our own realization.

Parallel Teachings of Two Buddhist Texts

In a very important Nyingma text, the *Trilogy of Natural Liberation* (Tib. *Rang grol skor gsum*) written by the renowned scholar Longchenpa (Tib. *Klong chen rab 'byams pa*) (1308-1363), the entire Nyingma tradition is condensed into three profound teachings: (1) Natural Liberation of the Mind-Itself (Tib. *sems nyid rang grol*); (2) Natural Liberation of *Dharmata* (Tib. *chos nyid rang grol*) and (3) Natural Liberation of Equanimity (Tib. *mnyam nyid rang grol*).

Let us briefly review the terms above. In this context, mind-itself refers to *tathagatagarbha-alayavijnana*, the ground of awakening and delusion. *Dharmata* refers to unconditioned truth, the true nature of reality, from which samsara and nirvana arise. Finally, equanimity refers to the Buddha nature realized by the bodhisattvas through progressing along various grounds; it is also referred to as the primordially pure *tathagatagarbha*.

These three profound teachings are parallel to the *tathagatagarbha-alayavijnana* doctrine described in the *Lankavatara Sutra*, which is considered to be an important Indian Mahayana Buddhist text. When Bodhidharma transmitted these teachings to his close disciple Huike (487-593) in China, he handed him the *Lankavatara Sutra* in four fascicules, or scrolls. Later, when Huike himself expounded the contents of the sutra, he repeatedly lamented after each lecture, "So sad. After four generations, I can foretell these teachings will become a mere concoction of names and intellectual concepts." Sure enough, four generations after Huike, his prophecy came true. Huineng and Shenxiu were among the best scholars of the final generation of the Lanka school. But after these two scholars, the teachings of the *Lankavatara Sutra* were reduced to mere intellectual studies. Scholars turned their attention to comprehending it on an intellectual level. Waves of academic terms and concepts were created by different schools, trying to adapt the meaning of the text to their own disciplines. The tenet of the *tathagatagarbha* doctrine – the essential meaning of the entire sutra – was then buried under an avalanche of concepts. Through the fog of confused intellectual interpretations, disciples were unable to decipher its inner meaning, and, therefore unable to apply the simple teachings of the doctrine to return to the liberating state of primordially pure *tathagatagarbha*.

If we tried to interpret the *Lankavatara Sutra* without any grounding in the doctrine of *tathagatagarbha*, the entire sutra would appear in disarray. It would seem like a series of incoherent, disjointed narrations adapted from intermixing theories. The teachings of the *Lankavatara Sutra* form part of the doctrinal foundations of the Nyingma School. These teachings can be organized into three sections: (1) an overview of the *tathagatagarbha* doctrine; (2) teachings on realizing *tathagatagarbha* through isolating defilements; and (3) teachings on returning *tathagatagarbha-alayavijnana* back to its primordial state of *tathagatagarbha*, the basis wisdom. The *Lankavatara Sutra* can be seen as the compendium of the *tathagatagarbha* doctrine. The entire sutra revolves around the teachings on *tathagatagarbha*. When we reach an understanding of *tathagatagarbha* as its foundation, the intricacies of the text will unravel.

To sum up: *tathagatagarbha* is the primordially pure ground. Primordially pure means that it has been pure since the dawn of time, and its purity is not fortuitously created. It is free from any elaboration. Because it is so pure, it is open to all possibilities. Like the sun, which naturally emits light and energy, primordially pure *tathagatagarbha* naturally manifests nirvana. Confined by delusion, however, *tathagatagarbha* is in the state of *alayavijnana* (all-basis consciousness). *Tathagatagarbha* is like a vast, calm ocean. The storms of our delusions cause huge waves to arise, which obscure the clear nature of *tathagatagarbha*. We see samsara rather than nirvana. In order to achieve liberation from the bonds of samsara, we must recognize the nature of mind-itself, which we do by overcoming delusion. This process of freeing ourselves from the chains of delusion is called natural liberation because we are returning ourselves to our natural liberated state. It is also sometimes called self-liberation because we liberate ourselves.

When we have attained liberation of the mind-itself, we have realized *tathagatagarbha*. This is not the ultimate realization, however. At the moment when the mind-itself is liberated, we abide simultaneously both in the *dharmata* and in everyday conditioned reality, where we are bound by space and time. Abiding in the *dharmata* is a new level of experience. In addition to the experience of the naturally arising pure and impure appearances, we will also recognize an unprecedented immaculate purity.

We need to further our practice to attain natural liberation of *dharmata*. When we attain natural liberation of *dharmata*, we abide in the state of equanimity or non-duality. In that state, we are completely free from dualistic thought. We realize that all phenomena, whether pure or impure, are mere self-arising appearances of the *dharmata*. We then acquire a deeper realization of *tathagatagarbha*. The previous level of realization, the natural liberation of the mind-itself, is the realization of the *Nirmanakaya* (Emanation body) of *tathagatagarbha*. This level of realization is the realization of the *Sambhogakaya* (Enjoyment body) of *tathagatagarbha*.

Abiding in the state of equanimity is not the same as having realized the Liberation of Equanimity, because while we are abiding in the state of equanimity, we are constrained by its limitations. However, at this high level of attainment, we are already bodhisattvas, having attained the eighth to tenth grounds of the bodhisattva's path to full enlightenment or Buddhahood. We need to practice unceasingly until we attain the Liberation of Equanimity, the ultimate realization. When we have attained Liberation of Equanimity, we have reached Buddhahood, and thus realized the *Dharmakaya* of *tathagatagarbha*, the ultimate realization of the primordially pure, unchanging *tathagatagarbha* – the essence of all wondrous possibilities. This is free from all reference points, free even from the reference of emptiness.

In this chapter, we have explained various technical terms and concepts, and revealed their inner meanings and interrelatedness. Although they may appear very technical and dry, these terms are prerequisites to the understanding of the practice of the six bardos, If we just want to enjoy beautiful flowers in someone else's garden, there is no need for us to go to great lengths to identify whether the flowers are staminate or carpellary, for instance. However, if we want to grow these same flowers from seed in our own garden, it is necessary that we acquaint ourselves with the related botanical terms in order to understand their propagation in sufficient depth. For our Dharma practice to flower fully, we need to understand the terminology of natural liberation, dry and technical though it may be. Greater effort at the beginning promises greater results at the end.

CHAPTER 6

The Six Bardos

THE *BARDO THODOL* WAS ONE OF THE FIRST Tibetan Buddhist texts to be published in the West, and is still one of the best known. It is a collection of various teachings on the "after death" experience. It was first translated into English by Kazi Dawa Samdup, edited by W. H. Y. Evans-Wentz, and published as *The Tibetan Book of The Dead* in 1927.[1] Since then, there have been many other translations, the most recent one being that of Gyurme Dorje.[2]

The bardo has been an enduring topic for those interested in looking beyond our phenomenal world. How well do we understand the meaning of bardo? By its most fundamental definition, bardo means an intermediate or in-between state. The term usually refers to an interim state of existence occurring immediately after death but before rebirth. Because the bardo is an in-between state following physical death, and can thus hardly be proven beyond doubt, it is sometimes mystically interpreted as a spirit or ghost state, and with the bardo beings being confused with spirits or ghosts.

In our Dharma practice, however, we are not too concerned with whether bardo beings are spirits or not. Rather, we use the concept of the bardo as a way of training ourselves in natural liberation. In natural liberation through the six bardos, the meaning of bardo is expanded to refer to six different phases in our lives. There is a specific meditation practice for each phase. In a practical sense, the practices of the six bardos can solve many of our daily problems, bringing harmony and joy to our everyday lives. More importantly, however, the practices provide the keys to unlock the meaning of naturally arising, opening the doors to our ultimate liberation.

Living life after life in samsara, we experience fleeting moments of these naturally arising phenomena. When a certain phenomenon arises physically, we call

---

1   Evans-Wentz, W.Y. (ed.) (1927) *Tibetan Book of the Dead: or, The After-Death Experiences on the Bardo Plane.* Lama Kazi Dawa-Samdup (translator). Oxford: Clarendon Press (Reissued 1960).

2   Coleman, Graham and Jinpa, Thupten (eds). *Meditations on Living, Dying, and Loss: The Essential Tibetan Book of the Dead.* Gyurme Dorje (translator). London: Penguin Books, 2005.

it birth. When it ceases to exist in our physical world, we call it death. The phenomenon of birth is analogous to the first appearance of an image on a television screen. That image fades, to be replaced by another and yet another. The images change constantly. When the final image is projected, illusory appearance ends, and we have what we call death. At the time of broadcast, to those watching the screen, the succession of images appears to be presenting a real and materially substantial world. To those who less engrossed in the program, and afterwards, the illusory nature of television projection is easily recognized.

If we loosen our hold on the appearances and disappearances that occur in our samsaric world, we will quickly realize that birth and death are merely different phases of continuous being. The appearance of a phenomenon, which we refer to as birth, has no independent reality; neither does its disappearance, which we call death, mean a complete end to its existence. The formats of appearance and disappearance are not the same, yet their natures are not different. In terms of the existence of a phenomenon, its appearance in this world is obviously different than its disappearance. In this sense, appearance and disappearance are not the same. However, because the natures of both appearance and disappearance are illusory, neither are they different. The phenomena of birth and death can only be described in terms of an interdependent relationship.

The Six Bardos

Buddhist thinkers long ago saw through the illusion of three-dimensional space and one dimensional time and re-conceptualized our lives as a series of phases of living and dying. They established the six bardos – six naturally arisen states of being. The six bardos are as follows:

> The bardo of living (Tib. *skye gnas bar do*)
> The bardo of dreams (Tib. *rmi lam bar do*)
> The bardo of meditation (Tib. *fbsam gtan bar do*)
> The bardo of dying (Tib. *'chi'i kha bar do*)
> The bardo of *dharmata* (Tib. *chos nyid bar do*)
> The bardo of becoming (Tib. *srid pa bar do*)

The first three bardos represent the different states we experience during our lifetime, while the last three are to be experienced when we die. The experiential trainings of the six bardos not only include practices for us to do while we are living but also practices that mimic the different stages we will experience during our death and before our rebirth.

If the six bardos are mere hypotheses, not rooted in absolute certainty, why would practices based on the bardo teachings bring any benefits? We can answer this question from two different perspectives. First, from a worldly point of view, we can observe that every moment in our lives is actually dependent upon myriad suppositions. The most obvious ones are the concepts of time and space. Time is defined according to the rotational relationships between the earth and the sun. We construct a notion of time in which a complete rotation of the earth around the sun is a year. The earth also rotates on its axis; we call a complete rotation of the earth on its axis a day. Within this day, we have daylight and nighttime, the length of which vary according to the position of the earth on its elliptical orbit around the sun. In our modern world, we subdivide the day into 24 sections that we name hours, and further subdivide hours into minutes, minutes into seconds and so on. Without a concept of the measurability of time, we could not establish a calendar, and record the events of our world. We also have a concept of space as being three-dimensional; without it we would not have length, area and volume, and other spatial measures.

Postulating three bardo stages occurring from death to rebirth is similar to theorizing about the dimensions of time and space. It may not be provable, but it is serviceable. It is believed that the after-death bardo states exist in a space that is invisible to us, and also in a time that is experienced differently than ours. Even though our practice is based on unproven suppositions, if we put our heart into it, we will eventually see results. Buddhists usually refer to such suppositions as "skilful means" (Skt. *upaya*) as they bring sincere practitioners closer to true enlightenment. Doing the practices of the six bardos has proven to be extremely effective in bringing about the realization of natural liberation. The practices are like a map which, if followed faithfully, will lead to natural liberation. The realization of natural liberation transcends time and space, and renders differences in religious standpoints on the subject of death irrelevant. By simply following the map, we will learn the language of living and dying, in the process preparing ourselves to cope with our own death.

In his commentary in the 1960 reissue of the Evans-Wentz edition of *The Tibetan Book of the Dead*, Carl Jung highly praised the teachings, asserting that they contain "the quintessence of Buddhist psychological criticism...of an unexampled superiority."[3] Jung believed that the bardos practices were exceptionally

---

3   Jung, Carl in Evans-Wentz, W.Y. (ed.)., ibid.

incisive in revealing human psychological perspectives. This Dharma practice is just the right antidote to our deeply embedded psychological imbalances.

There is a second way to answer the question asked above as to why the bardo practices, based as they are on suppositions, would be of benefit. In this physical world, concepts and labels completely structure our everyday lives in ways that are beneficial to our survival. Without ideas of "fire" and "burning," how would we be able to protect ourselves from the "danger" fire represents? But often, due to our material grasping, we fail to see the limitations inherent in our concepts and labels; instead we confuse our conceptual world, the world we have labelled, as the ultimate concrete reality. We are not usually aware that we have created a hypothetical world we have then named. Ironically, those who have been trained to view the world through the lens of a specific profession may think that their training gives them insight into the world as it really is; their professional know-how blinds them to the true nature of reality.

Living and dying are mere labels attached to concepts in our dimension of time and space. However hard we try, if we perceive these labels while wearing the spectacles of material grasping, we will remain strongly attached to our lives, and fear the perceived reality of death. But if we remove those spectacles to see clearly beyond the limited vision they impose, we can be released from the prison of our deluded perceptions, and feel at ease with every moment of living and dying. When we leap beyond the boundaries of concepts and labels, we realize the primordial wisdom of the Buddha. By following the manual that is the practice of the six bardos, Dharma practitioners learn to transcend their own constraints. Following the map of the six bardos holds immeasurable benefits for us.

The Three Pairs

The practices of the six bardos are related to each other in a complementary way. Organizing them into three pairs makes the relationship clear:

> The bardo of living – The bardo of dying
> The bardo of dreams – The bardo of *dharmata*
> The bardo of meditation – The bardo of becoming

Each pair is intimately related, the first being the preparation stage and the second the realization stage. If, during our lifetime, we have gained experience in the practices of the bardos of living and dying, at the moment of death, even though we have not attained complete realization, our familiarity with the bardo of dying will help us attain liberation. For those of us who have accumulated sufficient merit in our past lives, and who have sharp intelligence and spiritual inclination in this one, it is possible to attain liberation during our lifetime through practicing the bardo of living. Those of us with lesser capabilities, however, need not be discouraged, as we still have the chance of attaining liberation upon the moment of death through the practice of the bardo of dying. However, if we have not practised assiduously during our lifetime, it will be extremely difficult, if not impossible, to attain liberation by depending the practice of the bardo of dying at the moment of death.

How is it we can complete the practice and attain liberation upon the moment of death although we cannot do this during our lifetime? In order to understand, we need to recognize the numerous inherent constraints imposed by our physical body and senses. When our body falls ill, it is difficult not to be influenced by our own senses. Our eyes, ears, tongue, nose and bodily senses will all send messages to us, affecting our feelings and powers of reason. We are not only constrained solely by these bodily senses, but also by time and space. Only from the moment of death to the moment we undergo rebirth, while we exist in the bardo state, are we temporarily relieved of such limitations. The first practice of each bardo pair establishes the foundation for the second, which can be completed much more easily upon or after the moment of death, when we are under fewer constraints.

The other two pairs of bardo practices have the same complementary relationship as the bardos of living and dying; the faithful practice of the six bardos leads to attainment of the Buddha bodies: the *Dharmakaya, Sambhogakaya* and *Nirmanakaya*. These three pairs of practices are the foundation of the realization of the three Buddha-bodies and the keys to natural liberation.

PART II

The Practice Instructions of the Six Bardos

Practice Instruction for the Bardo of Living (Part 1)

"A Pigeon Returning to its Nest" – the Realization of Primordial Abode

WE CAN NOW BEGIN THE PRACTICE of the six bardos. The first practice is the bardo of living. Living takes place in the stretch of time from the moment of birth until we take our last breath, which we ordinarily think of as the moment of death. In fact, the process of dying is complex and begins sometime before we take our last breath. We begin dying while we are still living. Furthermore, according to the teachings of Tibetan Buddhism, dying continues for some time after the last breath is exhaled. Thus what we think of as a lifetime contains both the bardo of living and the bardo of dying. One lifetime encompasses the complete experience of these two bardos. The practice of the bardo of living is described allegorically in the ancient texts as a pigeon returning to its nest. This metaphor has an outer and an inner meaning. In its outer meaning, the theme of grounding our practice is compared to the labours of a pigeon building its nest. Before a pigeon constructs its home, it must go through all the preparatory stages, such as looking for a suitable place and finding the necessary materials. After its nest is complete, it then has a cozy home to which it can return. In the same manner, in the practice of natural liberation through the six bardos, we must first attend to Dharma and contemplate its meaning before we can engage ourselves in meaningful practice.

The metaphor of a pigeon returning to its nest is also significant in the context of abode. Although the pigeon frequently leaves its nest, fluttering and cooing on roofs and gables and taking flight, eventually it will want to return to its nest – its real home. This is equivalent to our wandering in samsara. By engaging in Dharma practice, we will be able to return to our original home, our abode, which is the primordial ground of all naturally arisen phenomena. This is the inner meaning of the metaphor. In order to accommodate different levels of practitioners, it is common in Vajrayana to have several explanations of the same metaphor. Besides an outer meaning, a teaching may have an inner, a secret and also a very secret meaning. Readers need to be careful not to misinterpret the meanings as being incompatible. The outer meaning of a pigeon returning to its nest is fairly straightforward. In the following section, we further discuss its inner meaning.

Illusory World

The illusory world is a world of virtual reality. Those of us who play simulation computer games are already familiar with a form of virtual reality. The game software enables us be actors in an artificial three-dimensional world. Players adopt an appearance and a personality that exists only within the game. Virtual reality is also used as a training technology, for example, giving would-be physicians a taste of the reality that awaits them when they actually begin treating real people. However, players and would-be physicians know when they have stepped outside the virtual reality of the game or the medical simulation. When we speak of the world that we inhabit as an illusory world, we are speaking of a virtual reality that is totally encompassing. We do not recognize that we are playing a game or engaging in a simulation of reality; we do not know that what we think of as reality is an illusion. We must be careful not to believe mistakenly that leaving computer-generated virtual reality for the so-called real world is equivalent to a pigeon returning to its nest! We may grasp onto what we think is real, but illusion is all that can be found. There is no place that is more real than the place where we are already. For the pigeon to truly return to its nest, we must return to the home within us, to the here and now, the primordial abode since beginning-less time. Through realizing that all appearances are but naturally arisen phenomena, illusory, and lacking inherent existence, we return instantly to the primordial ground from which all phenomena naturally arise. This primordial ground is the primordial abode of all naturally arisen phenomena. The primordial abode transcends time and space. It abides formlessly without limitation and nakedly without elaboration in the expanse of reality (Skt. *dharmadhatu*). The goal of practicing the bardo of living is to attain spontaneous realization of the different forms of illusory phenomena. Through recognizing their different illusory states, the realization of the meaning of naturally arisen phenomena will follow, enabling us to return to our primordial abode.

The practice instruction of the bardo of living involves two types of meditation training. One is the meditation on *shamatha* or tranquility; the other is the meditation on *vipassana* or higher insight. Tranquility meditation and insight meditation are practices common to many religions, varying only in their objects of focus, goals and intentions. The distinctiveness of Buddhist meditation lies in transcending different states of mind progressively, layer by layer, and making leaps into new states of awareness. We begin by deliberately conjuring a certain state of mind, intentionally grasping onto it as an objective of our meditation, and remaining focused on it single-pointedly. We then learn to forsake our new attainment, to let it go, in order to enter the new level of experience that follows. Buddhist meditation is not about an accumulation of Dharma know-how but rather a training that teaches us to progressively renounce our instinctive attachments, so that we can transcend layers upon layers of innate constraints, and thus make progress towards the attainment of natural liberation. When we understand this unique aspect of Buddhist meditation practice, the meanings of tranquility meditation and insight meditation are easily discerned.

Meditation Practice

When practising tranquility meditation, we begin by establishing an object of focus and then resting our mind on it, giving it our full attention. When our concentration lapses, we gently direct it back onto the object of meditation until we reach a state of single-pointed meditative engagement. Some meditation practices require the practitioner to drop the object of meditation and focus instead on *shunyata*, emptiness. Doing so, however, ironically makes emptiness itself the object of our focus. Our mind may experience some degree of spaciousness or other transcendental state, but we should not jump to the conclusion that we have realized emptiness. Such an experience does not equate to the realization of emptiness.

Insight meditation involves transcending layers and layers of boundaries that circumscribe our ability to see the ultimate nature. The intention is to achieve some breakthrough; therefore, the meditative absorption of tranquility meditation is not necessary. Generally speaking, the goal of insight meditation is to realize emptiness. However, as with tranquility meditation, if we struggle to realize emptiness in our meditation session, we will not find it easy to achieve our objective. If our minds become obsessed with grasping a concept called emptiness, which is itself beyond such a label, how can emptiness possibly be realized?

Although we have explained tranquility meditation and insight meditation in different terms, they are actually complementary and interdependent. From one state of awareness, another arises. We should not label one state of awareness as more important than another. If we strive to focus our mind in the first state of meditative absorption, the second meditative state will arise. Conversely, when the practitioner's goal is to focus on the second meditative state, the first arises. Of the two aspects of meditative practice, tranquility meditation focuses more on the arising of certain states of meditative absorption, whereas insight meditation puts more importance on transcending states of mind. For the sake of simplicity, tranquility meditation and insight meditation are usually taught separately, but in fact they are like the palm and back of the same hand and, as such, are one and inseparable. To practise tranquilly and insight meditation according to the practice of the bardo of living, we must fully understand that the two aspects of meditation are complementary and interdependent in transcending different stages of our innate obstructions. Only then will our meditation be vigorous and fruitful. Otherwise, even if we sat in a perfect lotus position for aeons, we would make little progress except for minor improvements in our posture!

The Natural Liberation of the Foundation

The practice instruction of the bardo of living is also termed the natural liberation of the foundation. Foundation refers to our *alayavijnana* or all-basis consciousness. It is the root of our samsaric existence. When the bardo being enters the womb of its mother to begin the process of rebirth, it is the *alayavijnana* that enters first; when we die, it is last to leave the body. All beings in samsara are bound under the direction of their *alayavijnana*. The main function of the *alayavijnana* is to store impressions of all the virtuous and non-virtuous deeds occurring over the course of our countless lifetimes. These impressions form the seeds of future actions. In itself, the *alayavijnana* is neither virtuous nor non-virtuous; it is simply a storehouse (without concrete reality). Our living and dying are all subject to the command of the *alayavijnana*. Hence, the liberation of the *alayavijnana,* the foundation of our samsaric experience, is a practice to naturally liberate our mind.

The Yogacara tradition of Tibetan Buddhism offers the most in-depth explanation of the *alayavijnana* in its instruction that our *alayavijnana* originates mainly from our deluded subject-object dichotomy, which segregates the apprehender from the apprehended. But what is the meaning of this subject-object dichotomy – the apprehender and the apprehended? When we watch a magnificent sunrise, through our sense of sight, we apprehend the beauty of the first light.

We are the subject, the apprehender, while the beautiful dawn is the object being apprehended. The apprehender is the subject arising from our ego, our I, and the apprehended is all phenomena external to our I. While we are living under the constraints of this domain of time and space, there is never any moment when we are not bound by the delusions imposed by our subject-object dichotomy. We cannot argue that it is wrong to have this subject-object dichotomy. All beings rely on their faculties of discrimination between self and other to survive. The problem lies in our mistaken grasping of the phenomena established through this dichotomy as solidly existent. This reinforces the importance of the I while relegating all other phenomena external to the I as secondary. It solidifies the reality of what we apprehend through our senses so that what is being apprehended appears as concretely real and independently existent. Our delusion blinds us every moment from recognizing that the true nature of all phenomena is naturally arisen from the primordial ground. Thus, in order to attain liberation of the *alayavijnana*, we must first realize the delusions that arise from our subject-object dichotomy. We must recognize that these dichotomized appearances – we the apprehender and them, the apprehended – are mere illusions, like reflections in a mirror. We then can be instantly liberated from the bounds imposed by our *alaya*, and live at ease in this dichotomized, illusive world. We can thus attain the natural liberation of the a*layavijnana*.

The practice of the bardo of living counters our grasping of the subject-object dichotomy. It is the antidote to our grasping of the subject and the object, the I versus all external phenomena. We can summarize the practice instruction of the Bardo of living as follows:

- Its goal is to attain the natural liberation of the *alayavijnana*
- Its means is to realize the illusory nature of both external phenomena and our inner consciousness.
- Its method is to progressively transcend different states of mind to attain the above realization.
- Its attainment is the realization that all phenomena, including ourselves, resemble myriad reflections in a mirror. They are mere naturally arisen phenomena of the primordial ground.
- If we consider all naturally arisen phenomena as Emanation bodies, then the natural liberation of *alaya* is to realize

that all phenomena are naturally arisen Emanation bodies.
From this, we realize the faculty of the expanse of reality
(*dharmadhatu*).

Having understood these points, we are now ready to begin our practice of the
bardo of living.

CHAPTER 8

Practice Instruction for the Bardo of Living (Part 2)

VERY OFTEN, THE PRACTICE OF TRANQUILITY MEDITATION is not as easy as we expect. Frequently, it is not the meditation itself that is difficult, but rather the diligence required to commit to such an ongoing practice is hard to maintain. Inevitably, after three or four weeks of practice, beginners, though initially very enthusiastic, find themselves coming up with many excuses not to practice, and begin to slack off. Eventually, practice comes to a total halt. Tibetan Buddhist practitioners describe this impediment as the "*mara* of hindrances" (*maras* are projections of our delusions); in fact, failing to practice is mostly an internal obstacle that can be surmounted with some determination.

When I first began practising Tibetan Buddhism in 1964, I too occasionally succumbed to this *mara* of hindrances. Then I set a rule for myself: I would meditate on my way to work. So, on my tram ride to work, I would find a seat that was conducive to tranquility meditation. As soon as I sat down, I absorbed myself in a single-pointed meditative state and meditated for at least 20 minutes. I did this each day. After persisting in this practice for a period of time, I managed to pacify my *mara*. However, there was a downside to meditating on the tram. I could not sit cross-legged in the proper seven-point posture, which is extremely beneficial for meditators. To compensate, I set aside a little time each day to practise while sitting properly in the seven-point posture. I persevered with the practice for nearly 20 years.

Seven-point Posture of Vairocana

The cross-legged posture is commonly called the "seven-point posture of Vairocana." It is said to have been conveyed by Vairocana himself, and is thus named after him. The seven points refer to seven key aspects of this posture. There are two different methods of teaching this seven-point practice. In essence, however, they are actually quite similar. The traditional teaching is as follows:

1. Sit in the lotus position, with the feet placed on opposite thighs. If this is too difficult, you can choose to sit in a half-lotus position with one foot placed on the opposite thigh. If it is still difficult, you can simply sit in a regular cross-legged position.

2. Straighten your spine and sit upright.

3. Place your right hand on top of your left hand, in a medi-tative *mudra*, and rest your hands below your navel. Both hands should be flat, palms facing upwards. Your thumbs should be relaxed, barely touching, forming a straight line above the palm. If your hands are too tight, with thumbs pressing tightly against each other, they will point out-wards, creating a triangle instead of a straight line.

4. Lower your eyelids, keeping your eyes half-open. Focus your eyes at a 45-degree angle to the ground. A common mistake is to close the eyes completely. This is a serious mistake, which can lead to emotional imbalances. If this happens, it will be difficult for you to progress to more advanced meditation.

5. Bring your chin in slightly, but not so low as to touch your neck. Your back should remain straight, with the neck slightly bent in a relaxed position.

6. Place the tip of your tongue lightly on your hard palate. Remember to relax. Too tight a posture will cause a sore throat. Placing the tongue this way will naturally increase the flow of saliva. Swallow it slowly and gently as needed.

7. Slightly retract your lower abdomen towards your back, but remember not to hold it too tightly.

Adhering to these seven key points is of paramount importance in meditative practice. According to Tibetan Buddhist teachings, a proper posture with a straight spine will automatically straighten the channels, allowing the winds to flow properly within the body. When these winds are flowing properly, you can naturally focus and rest single-pointedly in meditative absorption (Skt. *samadhi*). In *samadhi*, the practitioner's body is in a state of total relaxation, feeling as light as if it were weightless. If you feel any physical discomfort, your body may be too tense and tight; it is important to remember to relax.

Simple Meditation Practice

If we are committed practitioners, we should practise in the formal seven-point posture of Vairocana. However, those with a hectic lifestyle and who have difficulty finding time to relax can make use of their break times to do some simple meditation practice. Simply sit upright and relaxed in a chair with good back support, let go of your daily worries, and listen to your own breathing. By paying attention to your breathing for thirty seconds, you will begin to hear the rhythm of your heartbeat. By listening to the soft beat of your pulse for another thirty seconds, you will soon hear blood flowing gently throughout the body, like spring water running downstream, infused with energy and life. Rest yourself in this vigorous serenity for another two minutes. In time you may experience surprising discoveries. When I do this simple practice, I feel overwhelmingly re-freshed, as if I have just awakened from a deep, nurturing sleep.

If, when meditating, you yawn, it is a sign that you have been over-exerting yourself and are feeling fatigued. If you cough or your throat feels sore, it may be an indication of a respiratory tract infection. If you feel movement of your intestine, or even hear sounds from your abdomen, it suggests problems with your digestive system. If you place yourself in meditative absorption for several minutes as described above, you will be able to determine your own health problems! Do not be disappointed if you do not experience anything during your first few meditations. Simply enjoy the process and meditate on this three to four times a day. Within a week, you should notice a big difference in your experience.

Even for a committed practitioner, one need not to stretch the tranquility medi-tation into a long session. Sometimes, it is more beneficial to keep the sittings short, from 15 to 20 minutes each, and increase the frequency to 10 or even 20 times a day. We call these "short frequent practices." Short sessions can prevent practitio-ners from forcing themselves to meditate beyond their zone of comfort. Forcing yourself to engage in long, dull meditative sessions will only make your body and mind tense, causing fatigue and preventing your thoughts from settling. In the long run, it could lead to a state of listless doldrums. Meditating with closed eyes or with poor motivation could also lead to similar unintended and unwelcome results.

Stone Gazing

The formal practice of tranquility meditation often begins with placing our mind on stone or wood. We call it stone gazing for short. To do it, begin by sitting in the seven-point posture (a small cushion may be placed under the spine for more comfort). Place a pebble, or small piece of wood, in front of yourself as the object of meditation. The stone should not be too reflective or colourful; a plain oval pebble is ideal. In a relaxed manner, keep your eyes focused on the stone. Do not stare or tense the eyes. Try looking at the stone as you would gaze at a small bird about to take wing, or as a child seeing a fully blossomed flower for the first time and absorbed in wondrous admiration. In this way, your gaze will be neither too lax nor too tense. Acquiring this attentive yet calm gazing skill is especially important nowadays; we call it "casual gazing with keen alertness." Stone gazing is called "tranquility meditation with signs"; it is so named because in the practice, we focus on a physical object, which we term a sign. It is a beginning practice.

Casual gazing with keen alertness has application outside of a formal meditation practice. In the modern information age, many of us must fix our eyes on a computer screen for several hours in one sitting. Such close attention can strain our eyes tremendously and may even numb our minds. Why? Because we often forget to relax our eyesight. I teach my students to use the casual gazing technique while reading intensively on a computer screen. The students have all increased their reading comprehension admirably while reducing tension. The practice has two steps:

1. Imagine the background of the computer screen as a clear blue sky. Read the words or pictures as if they are clouds and rainbows in the sky. At first, it may seem difficult for you to concentrate on the meaning of the words while simultaneously thinking of them as clouds and rainbows. However, if you patiently practise this exercise for three or four days, you will quite easily become accustomed to it.
2. Keep imagining that the words or pictures on the screen are clouds and rainbows while responding to them with your bodily senses; use your nose, mouth, neck, shoulders, chest, even with your lungs. Become absorbed in them.

In our everyday lives, we often gaze in a relaxed but alert manner. We may do it while watching birds take flight or observing a bee pollinate a flower. A parent who cooks dinner while watching her child play at her side is also engaging in a kind of relaxed but attentive gazing. We can apply casual gazing while working, watching a movie or reading a book, allowing our eyes to perform optimally without being stressed.

Proper Breathing

When we breathe, we should allow our breathing to settle peacefully and naturally; we should not attempt to control its rate. In Buddhism, breath is often referred to as wind. When our wind becomes subtle, long and slow, similar to the breathing of a tortoise, we enter a state of quiet absorption. In Daoism, a special breathing technique is taught to make our regular breathing slower and more subtle, like that of a tortoise. It is believed that this state of "tortoise absorption" can prolong our lives. However, in tranquility and insight meditation, be it stone gazing or another practice, we do not strive to attain a state of tortoise absorption. Instead, we focus on the object of our meditation, and allow our breathing to rest naturally in the state of absorption. Like a heavy cloud that is slowly and naturally dispersed into traces of feathery cirrus, drifting through the sky, our wind becomes subtle and clear.

No sooner do we manage to settle our mind, however, than it starts to wander. We want our mind to remain settled, our gaze to remain focused, and our body to remain relaxed, but thoughts arise against our will, without the slightest conscious effort. Sometimes the thoughts bring back reminiscences so powerfully vivid that we are swept off balance. The more distracted we are, the harder we fix our gaze upon the stone. To remedy this situation, we can try counting our breaths – either our inhalations or exhalations, but not both – as we gaze at the pebble. When distraction arises, we can bring our attention back to this breath-counting exercise. Eventually our wandering thoughts will settle and our breathing will become more subtle. If we are so distracted that nothing helps, it is better to halt our meditation session and return to it at another time.

There are other types of tranquility meditation in addition to tranquility meditation with signs, but before I elaborate further, I would like to turn to the topic of post-meditation practice. The essential objective of meditation is to train our mind. During formal meditation, we learn to focus our mind resolutely on the object of meditation. But if we immediately slips back into our ordinary busy routine once we have completed the formal session, we have not fully achieved this goal. Outside of our formal sitting sessions, it is important to maintain the state of mind generated during meditation.

Closed meditation retreats can be very helpful for practitioners endeavouring to maintain the same state of mind after formal sittings. During retreats, external distractions are kept to a minimum. Practitioners can even choose to refrain from conversation. Under such ideal conditions, we can devote every moment of our day to Dharma practice, thus making it easier to maintain the states of mind generated during formal sitting sessions. For most of us, however, it is quite impractical to abandon all worldly affairs and enter a closed retreat. Besides, a closed retreat requires the careful guidance of a guru. It is more practical for most people to learn to maintain the same meditative state of mind as they go about their daily lives. Maintaining the meditative experience following a meditative session involves two imperatives. One, we must stay mindful, and keep our minds from indulging in idle discursive thought. Two, we must apply our mindfulness to our daily lives. The post-meditation experience is not a state of obliviousness or inattention to the world around us. To the contrary, practitioners who bring the meditative mind to their everyday lives live vigorous, fully engaged lives with a fresh new perspective.

The practice of meditating with signs helps us to loosen our innate grasping in our daily lives. It trains us to look at life naturally with a casual gaze, in tune with our mind and heart. With such training of the mind, our powers of observation will increase tremendously, allowing the appreciation of fine details that others would not normally detect. For example, while examining a flower, we may notice the beauty of delicate patterns in the petals. At the same time, we may discover a sweet, intoxicating scent which we never noticed before. This stage of the practice may induce two different psychological responses. It may cause us to focus excessively on beauty, or alternatively, on ugliness. In the latter case, even the tiniest flaw could become the centre of focus, revealing a tendency to concentrate on the negative. There is danger here, as preoccupation with the negative is the biggest roadblock in meditation practice. If we find we are obsessing about flaws and faults, we should try to rediscover the beauty within imperfection. It may be helpful to remember that to the collector, odd-looking objects are often more interesting, and more beautiful, than those that conform to conventional ideals of beauty.

When our minds are in tune with our eyes, and we can always look at all phenomena in our everyday lives casually, we have achieved what is meant by casual gazing. Dedicate a non-working day to practising eight to ten sessions of stone gazing. Spend the time in between meditation sessions making some observations about the world around you: look at the street outside; watch the passers-by. Observe your inner responses. Have you transcended the ordinary world around you? If you have, you will have experienced an indescribable but definite change: your entire world will have become auspiciously different.

CHAPTER 9

Practice Instruction for the Bardo of Living (Part 3)

IN ORDER TO ADVANCE from tranquility meditation with signs to both tranquility meditation without signs and insight meditation, there are some interim practices with which we need to familiarize ourselves. In this chapter, we will discuss three of them. As a foundation to these practices, we must open our hearts to the qualities of the phenomena around us. In the last chapter, we began the formal practice of tranquility meditation with stone gazing, choosing a simple pebble as the object of meditation. The next step in tranquility meditation with signs is to choose objects that appear interesting and lively. By taking in their boundless energy, we familiarize ourselves with the positive qualities to all phenomena, and establish a good foundation for two further practices: that of placing our mind between our eyebrows and that of placing it at our heart. For the former of these two practices, we visualize a pure, luminous white drop the size of a pea between our eyebrows and rest our attention on it. When we are able to do this, we then advance to the latter meditation, that of placing our mind at our heart. We begin by visualizing our body as a puffed-up sack, similar to an inflated balloon. At the heart of the sack, we visualize a luminous, blue-orange flame, like that of an oil lamp. We focus our attention on the flame, while remembering to relax. The practices of stone gazing and gazing on a more complex object make us aware of the vitality of our external environment; the two practices of placing our mind between our eyebrows and at our heart are ways to observe the same vitality from our own subtle awareness. Our concentration has become more subtle; instead of gazing casually with our eyes, we are focusing casually with our mind. We are moving from a visual gazing practice to that of a mental concentration practice where we visualize with our mind in a focused yet relaxed manner.

Meditation on Holy Beings

When we have some experience of the above practices, we can progress to the next level of meditation practice wherein we visualize holy beings. Although this meditation originates from Buddhist traditions, it is not bounded by any faith. Adherents of different faiths may visualize whomever or whatever is appropriate to their faith tradition. For Buddhists, it is most common to visualize Buddha Shakyamuni or the compassionate Avalokiteshvara. When we meditate on holy beings or objects, it is important that we remember that their essence is pure, luminous and empty of inherent existence. We are not trying to project an idealized image or object for worship; on the path of liberation, having a mind locked in idol worship, or idolatry, is just another form of grasping and attachment. A mind grasping after the inherent existence of even a virtuous being or object will naturally also reify the external world, categorizing humankind into believers and non-believers, friends and enemies, and so on, and will inevitably extend the categorization process to encompass all other phenomena. Such blindness to the true nature of reality can result in extremist views. However, through the merits we ascribe to holy beings and objects, we can recognize the luminosity that pervades all space and time.

Tranquility Meditation without Signs

At this stage, I would like to point out one problem with meditation practice that is frequently encountered by beginners. Often, the harder we try to concentrate, the more our discursive thoughts seem to overwhelm our mind. Actually, though it may seem otherwise, when we notice our mind begin to wander, we are putting casual gazing or casual focus into effect. Before engaging in meditation practice, we had no direct experience of our minds; we did not notice our mind stream, where our thoughts appear and disappear like waves on water. Through practising tranquility meditation, however, our awareness has become sharpened. Because of our heightened sense of awareness, we are suddenly aware of an endless ocean of thoughts, churning restlessly and unceasingly in our minds. How then can we settle our wandering mind? We can pacify it as we might control a horse we are riding. When our mind starts to wander, we tighten the reins and gently guide it back to the intended object of meditation. At other times, we may loosen the reins and allow our thoughts to flow freely. By practising consistently and alternating between concentration and relaxation, we will eventually bring our wandering minds under control. At this point, unbidden thoughts will dissolve naturally as they arise, and our mind will remain settled and undisturbed. This kind of meditation practice, wherein we calm our discursive thoughts, is termed "tranquility meditation without signs." Without signs means that the practitioner transcends the signs, such as stone, white drops, and holy beings and objects previously used as the object of meditation. There is no need for them. When our mind is settled, our discursive thoughts naturally dissolve; furthermore, the solidity of the signs used as the object of meditation does the same, allowing our mind to settle in the vast empty space. It is often easier to settle our minds through tranquility meditation without signs than it is through tranquility meditation with signs; a formless rein is very effective in restraining the uncontrolled horse of our mind.

Tranquility meditation without signs is often misunderstood to be a meditation on realizing emptiness. This is a huge mistake. Focusing on empty space is very different from realizing emptiness. When we focus our attention on empty space, empty space is the object of our meditation. We must not confuse empty space with emptiness-itself. Similarly, if we consider the combustible nature of wood, we should not confuse a state of combustion of the wood with the nature of combustion itself. They are different. We can develop a similar analogy with water. In its liquid form, water flows. But a state of flowing water is not the nature of flowing itself.

Insight Meditation

The Buddhist term "emptiness" does not mean nothingness. Meditating under an incorrect view of emptiness will certainly lead to confusion and may also lead to solipsism, nihilism or essentialism. In the this section, we discuss the correct way to meditate on emptiness, which is insight meditation in the bardo of living. The practice of insight meditation involves three practices:

1. Recognizing the mind-itself;
2. Searching for the mind-itself; and
3. Ascertaining, or definitively identifying, the nature of primordial awareness or *rigpa* (Tib. *rig pa*).

We must not be alarmed by these complicated phrases. When we first encounter these instructions, they often sound unattainably difficult, but they are actually very simple. There is no need to feel overwhelmed by them.

Recognizing the Mind-Itself

Let us begin by recognizing the manifestations of the mind-itself. The mind expresses or manifests itself unceasingly and spontaneously every moment. We are so preoccupied with ourselves, however, that we have never noticed the way these manifestations appear. Instead, we mistakenly identify them as our own independent thoughts, words and actions. The expressions of our mind are analogous to reflections in a mirror or ripples in a pond. When people stand in front of a mirror, they notice their images, rather than the nature of the mirror itself. When people observe water flowing in a river, they notice the ripples and waves rather than the nature of the water itself. In turn, when we observe ourselves, we only notice our body, speech and mind busy in action. Rarely do we realize that the ground from which all our actions arise is the mind-itself.

Longchenpa (Tib. *Klong chen pa*), an important master of the Nyingma school, gave us an analogy that helps us understand the manifestation of the mind-itself. A child sees his dirty face in a mirror, and tries to clean it by wiping the mirror's reflection with his dirty hands. Seeing this, his mother tries to help, using a clean cloth to wipe the reflection of his grimy face. However, the mother really knows that in order to see a clean image in the mirror, she should be wiping her child's face, not the reflection. Wiping the mirror's reflections in hope of a clean face is like looking into empty space to find emptiness-itself; it is a futile endeavour. Just as empty space should not be confused with emptiness-itself, so a mind free of thoughts should not be misconstrued as a manifestation of the mind-itself, for it is not.

Some Buddhist schools recommend that the practitioner should first establish an intellectual understanding of the correct view of emptiness, and then meditate accordingly. This method of practice has a major drawback: the practitioner could easily fall into the trap of the limitations of his own preconceptions, and find himself unable to transcend beyond his conceptual understanding to observe any ground beyond that which has been explained in words. Any explanation of emptiness is mere words and concepts, not its essence; following a conceptual path to realize a non-conceptual object is fraught with problems, and may severely hinder progress. If we become too comfortable with the act of cleaning the mirror, it is hard to break through the original misconception and realize that what is really needed is to clean our face. On the other hand, the Nyingma lineage would advise the practitioner to first clean her face; this way the mirror would naturally reflect a clean image. Accordingly, before pointing out the primordial ground, the Nyingma guru would first establish the meditation practice for his disciples to observe the natural manifestation of the mind-itself. When his disciples were well versed in their given practice, the guru would then give teachings on the ground, and lead them to the correct path. When we have no preconceptions of the nature of the ground, it is often easier to leap beyond our boundaries and directly realize the nature of the ground through direct meditation experience. Eventually, the practitioner will realize the mind-itself. For instance, by observing the state of natural intrinsic luminosity, she will realize that the manifestations of the mind-itself are empty in nature.

The meditation on natural intrinsic luminosity involves observing the *kati* channel at our heart. It resembles a small, clear, luminous, hollow crystal in the shape of a peppercorn slightly burst open. We meditate single-pointedly upon the *kati* channel until our mind achieves steady concentration. When that concentration is stable and growing, we can relax our focus and let the mind be at ease. As we alternate between concentration and relaxation, we observe spaces or gaps where we can see the nature of the mind-itself. This practice is technically called "observing the gap in between two thoughts." It requires very delicate and discerning observation.

What is the nature of the mind-itself like? An explanation is provided in the Dunhuang manuscript known as *Lidai fabao ji*. It is an important scripture in the Szechuan school of Chan, which later became the Baotang school, named after its original temple, the Baotang temple. It records the teachings of their master Wushang:

> Every December and January, thousands of monks, nuns, lay-men and laywomen gathered together at the sacred temple of Baotang to hear the teaching of Master Wushang. The Master first taught the people how to chant the name of the Buddha. Like an opera singer extending a note, he chanted the name of the Buddha in one long breath. When he stopped chanting, he said: In that moment, there is no reminiscence, no thought, no distraction. No reminiscence is the precept; No thought is the *samadhi*; No distraction is the wisdom. These three mottoes are the Dharani Gate, the gate to wisdom. These words of wisdom are the direct teaching of Bodhidharma, and not from Master Xin or Master Tang.[1]

Wushang emphasized that this chanting practice was transmitted directly from the matchless master Bodhidharma, and not from his own masters. This shows

---

1   Master Tang was the teacher of Wushang, while Master Xin was the teacher of Master Chixin. Nowadays, we refer to Wushang as Kim Heshang, because he was Korean and his birth name in Korean is Kim.

how precious and important the teaching is. In that one breath, from the beginning of chanting to its end, there exists precisely "a gap between two thoughts" – the thought of "chanting" and the thought of "stopping chanting." Only at this instance can we realize the meaning of no reminiscence, no thought and no distraction.

Bodhidharma's recitation practice is very similar to the Nyingma school's meditation practice on observing the gap between alternating states of concentration and relaxation. Through observing the gap between these two states, we can experience a moment of clarity free of the karmic imprints of our body, speech and mind. Only within these gaps are moments completely free from thoughts. Within these gaps mind-itself is manifest. A practice grounded on suppressing thoughts by merely "not thinking" will not reveal to the practitioner the true nature of the mind-itself. Neither can mind-itself be recognized according to any preconceived descriptions. Upon recognition of the mind-itself, intrinsic luminosity will naturally arise. This luminosity is not that of the *kati* channel but neither is it separated from it. In this special moment, we have attained *samadhi*, the state of luminous clarity, free from all concepts and elaboration. This is the secret meaning of the teaching.

Searching for the Mind-Itself

The second practice of insight meditation is searching for the mind-itself. There are two common misunderstandings. The first is that in searching for the mind-itself, we actually believe it is something external to us. Not so. Rather, the meditation teaches us the futility of looking for the mind-itself outside of our minds. In the meditation, we try to find the mind-itself somewhere and hold it in our meditation, but we discover the more we struggle to find it, the more elusive it becomes, leaving us in total confusion. As with a pond of clear water, which gets murkier the more a person stirs it, the more we look for our mind-itself, the harder it is to recognize its true nature. The second common misunderstanding comes from a misinterpretation of the phrase "A knife does not cut itself and a fire does not burn itself." Some people mistakenly conclude that the phrase means "The mind does not (or cannot) seek the mind-itself." In fact, it means that the practitioner should not to seek the mind-itself based on attainments that arise from that same state of mind because both are manifestations of the same state of awareness. Such intellectual activity is actually not conducive to our progress. When we engage in a search this way, we destroy the precious, animated openness of our mind. When we engage in the search for the mind-itself, we are actually making use of the faculties or inherent capabilities of our mind to search for its nature, i.e. the mind-itself. An object's nature and its faculties are very different. Here, we are not using a blade to cut itself or a flame to burn itself. Instead, we try to understand the nature of the knife itself through observing its inherent capability of cutting. Similarly, by observing fire's inherent capability of burning, we come to realize the nature of fire itself.

Engaging in a search for the mind-itself is similar to the practice of *koan*s in Zen Buddhism. In koan practice, the practitioner first places his mind in the empty space in front of him. Then, he observes whether the person who placed the mind and the mind-itself are one object, or whether they are in fact two separate objects. If they are indeed one thing, then is this oneness the mind? If they are indeed two separate things, then there must be two separate minds – one being in samsara and the other one on the path to Buddhahood.

Ascertaining the Nature of Primordial Awareness or *Rigpa*

The third practice of insight meditation is to ascertain the nature of *rigpa*. The goal is to seek primordial awareness, also sometimes referred to as naked awareness, intrinsic luminous awareness or, more technically, *rigpa*. Emptiness is an aspect of *rigpa* but they are not the same. According to the Nyingma school, *rigpa* is explained in three aspects: its essence, or nature, as being empty; its expression through manifestation or appearance as natural cognizance; and its faculties, or inherent capabilities, as infinite displays. Of the three aspects, the most difficult to realize is its nature being empty. Even in our everyday lives, we find it hard to discern the nature of things.

For example, we may ask ourselves, what is the nature of water? We could answer that it is a type of liquid that flows from high to low altitudes. It is composed of two hydrogen atoms and one oxygen atom. When it is calm, it reflects images perfectly, like a mirror; and when it moves, it creates ripples or even tidal waves. However, all these are merely descriptions of its expression or appearance, not its nature. We could elaborate further that water is a powerful solvent and can dissolve dirt. It is buoyant; we can float on it, and swim across its surface. It is home to coral reefs and countless species of fish. Even with such detailed descriptions, we have merely described the inherent capabilities of water; we have not been able to articulate its nature clearly in words. Although we are unable to describe the nature of the objects we encounter in our daily lives, this does not cause us any inconvenience. When we meet water, fire, wind or other natural or man-made items, it seems that all we need to know about them are their expressions and inherent capabilities. Through inference, we seem to comprehend their nature, but cannot articulate it in language. Their nature is beyond words, though not beyond thoughts or conscious comprehension. In other words, we rely on the appearance and inherent capabilities of an object to comprehend its nature. We have done this throughout our lives, and have accumulated a kind of working knowledge and wisdom about the world and its phenomena.

Before we try to realize emptiness, we must first determine the meaning of emptiness. Just as we should not claim to know the nature of water merely from looking at a pond, we should not conclude that we have realized emptiness merely by looking into empty space. Although we may often experience a certain calmness or spaciousness from such insight meditation, we should not hastily jump to conclude that this is a realization of emptiness. Fortunately, the Nyingma school offers a very practical approach to realizing emptiness. If we can realize the nature of water, fire, wind and the world around us through their appearances and capabilities, then we can similarly realize emptiness through its expressions and inherent capabilities. Because the realization of emptiness largely depends on our observation of its related aspects, the practice instruction of the bardo of living puts great emphasis on recognizing expressions of emptiness as natural cognizance and its inherent capability or faculty as display.

Natural cognizance is a component of the expressive aspect. It does not refer to the expression or form itself, but is the means through which expressions become discernible. Through this inherent distinguishable aspect, we differentiate one phenomenon from another. The Cittamatra school explains this distinguishable aspect from the perspective of our human consciousness, or more precisely, our discriminating faculties. The Nyingma school on the other hand extends the view beyond the perimeters of our ordinary conception. The Nyingma assert that since all phenomena can be discerned by our consciousness, they must possess an intrinsic element that enables us to identify them. This aspect inherent to all phenomena and appearances is natural cognizance. All things, whether external phenomena or inner awareness, have their natural cognizance. Even emptiness has its related natural cognizance. From our inner perspective, our inner consciousness, for example, our eye consciousness, is the natural cognizance of our *rigpa*. From the union of the natural cognizance of our inner consciousness with that of the external phenomena, we can distinguish one phenomenon from another. Natural cognizance is intrinsic not only to our eye consciousness and the appearances of physical objects; other consciousness, such as form, sound, smell, taste and touch, also have their natural cognizance. Furthermore, the natural cognizance of each consciousness may have further elaborations, depending on what is cognized. For example, with the ear consciousness, it could be a speech, a symphony or a storm that is cognized.

Natural cognizance of phenomena always adapts spontaneously to the particular realm of existence in which they appear. Different pools of the collective karma of sentient beings give rise to different realms of existence. In other words, in every realm of existence, a common collective karma is inherent within every sentient being in that realm. All the sentient beings of a particular realm have a common platform of cognition. For example, in our realm of time and space, we cognize iron as hard and cold. However, in another realm of time and space, the same metal may be considered differently, possibly as soft and malleable. The natural cognizance of iron of being hard in our realm will naturally adapt itself to the conditions of the other realm so that it is in harmony with it. The qualities of all phenomena are relative.

The aspect or faculty of inherent capability is known as "display." Display does not mean "manifestation" in this context. It means that the expanse of reality (*dharmadhatu*) has an inherent capability of allowing all phenomena to arise naturally. From Buddha's perspective, this inherent capability is his merit, or great compassion. From our perspective, it is the boundless vitality of all phenomena, which we call great bliss. At first glance, the meanings of great compassion and great bliss seem to be in conflict. In actuality, they both refer to the same inherent capabilities of the *dharmadhatu* – its inherent capability for infinite love, compassion and creation. Also, we need to understand that the aspect of emptiness, natural cognizance and display of phenomena are inseparable, and mutually dependent. They are inherent parts of *rigpa* just as fluidity, buoyancy and the boundless vitality of water are connate qualities of water.

In order to realize emptiness, we need to observe its related aspects, its expressions as natural cognizance and its inherent capabilities as display. When we first attain a special wisdom realizing emptiness, our mind is not completely mixed with the object. We need to further our practice to attain certainty of non-conceptuality. Once we realize the meaning of naturally arisen phenomena, we understand that there is no conceptual appearance on the pure ground of *rigpa*. Because of the spontaneous play of natural cognizance and unceasing display, phenomena appear to us as different and distinct. We conceptualize them with different names and labels, as fire seems clearly different from water. But on the pure ground of *rigpa*, all these conceptual appearances – whether appearing as being produced or having ceased to exist, whether coming or going, being the same or different, tainted or pure – will completely dissolve. All that appear on the immaculate ground of *rigpa* are naturally arisen magical displays, free from concepts and elaboration.

We rest the mind nakedly and steadily in its luminosity, without any contrivances. The luminous awareness that intrinsically arises is *rigpa*. All phenomena that appear distinct and real to our mind are but the boundless vitality of the *dharmadhatu* and the expression of its natural cognizance. In this unceasing display, abundant with intense liveliness, the luminosity of *rigpa* naturally permeates and pervades all space. When we are patient and practise insight meditation consistently, *rigpa* naturally arises. To supplement our insight meditation practice, the Dzogchen tradition has two additional practices, *togal* (Tib. *thod rgal*) "leap over" and *trekcho* (Tib. *khred chod*) "cutting through." Like insight meditation, the practices of *togal* and *trekcho* are instrumental in recognizing our mind-itself. Although the three practices are different, their goal is essentially the same: to recognize the natural manifestation of the mind-itself, upon which beginners should focus their efforts. By alternating between these complementary meditation practices, we will naturally gain insights and be able to understand the nature of mind-itself. Because the nature of the object of meditation is so subtle and hence easily misunderstood, it is important that we practise under the guidance of a qualified guru. We will discuss *togal* and *trekcho* in later chapters.

CHAPTER 10

Practice Instruction for the Bardo of Dreams (Part 1)

THE PRACTICE INSTRUCTION FOR THE BARDO OF DREAMS is a very important teaching; its main practice of clear light is considered to be especially profound and advanced. The practice is akin to illuminating a darkened room. During the course of life after life, we have lived behind a smokescreen of delusion, unable to see beyond it, as if we were trapped in a poorly lit room. The practice of clear light sweeps away our delusions, much as light that dispels darkness. Often, upon introducing this practice, the lineage guru will provide supplementary verbal training of an individual nature to his disciple. The main commitment upon receiving such direct verbal transmission is not, as might be thought, to keep the teaching secret, but to personalize it. Because each of us is unique and our responses to the practice will differ, the guru will supplement the instruction according to our individual needs. Although these chapters cannot offer personalized instructions, they can explain the principles behind these practices.

The teachings of the bardo of dreams are the keys to enlightenment and are extremely important for practitioners to understand.

The practice instruction of the bardo of dreams consists of three parts:

1. Daytime practice of the illusory body;
2. Night-time practice on dreaming; and
3. The concluding practice of clear light.

The daytime practice of the illusory body has two primary practices: one, the practice of illusory body, speech and mind; and two, the practice of pure illusory body. The first is a practice of recognizing the illusory nature of our body, speech and mind. The second is a practice of viewing appearances as spontaneous natural display, which is sometimes referred to as training in pure view. The purpose of illusory body practice is to liberate us from our grasping of ordinary appearances. This attainment is analogous to the state of mind of an illusory person leaving the scene of an illusion. As an example, take a magic show where in a magician conjures up an image of a person inhabiting a scene that is deceptively convincing. Imagine that one day, this illusory person has a chance to depart this illusory scene, and he chooses to leave. When he looks back, nothing looks quite the same as before. He looks at himself, and immediately realizes that his existence is merely an illusory appearance in an illusory world.

In Buddhism, phenomena are but the natural expression of primordial ground. These naturally arisen phenomena are like the illusory person and the illusory world in which he lives. To the illusory person, the phenomena of living and dying in his illusory world seem very real; only the magician realizes that those phenomena are illusory. Similarly, phenomena in our world appear solidly real to us, and only enlightened beings understand that they are but illusory appearances. The intention of the illusory body practice is to enable us to recognize our own illusory appearance. Once we realize this, we are spontaneously liberated from attachment to our I and the world of phenomena. When our mind is liberated from attachment to itself and the phenomenal world, it abides in a state of awareness similar to that which the magician's illusory person experiences when he leaves the world of illusion. We can call this experience the liberation of the mind-itself.

Illusory body practice is grounded in the practices of the bardo of living, as explained in the previous three chapters. Through the meditative experience we gain from practice of the bardo of living, we should acquire some insight into the three aspects of *rigpa*: its nature as empty, its expression as natural cognizance and its faculty as display. In addition, we may also have some experience in recognizing appearances as spontaneous displays of the mind-itself. Building on such attainments, we can deepen our realization through the practice of illusory body, speech and mind, as explained below.

The Daytime Practice of Illusory Body, Speech and Mind

The daytime practice of illusory body, speech and mind has three parts. The first part of the practice of illusory body, speech and mind is the practice of recognizing appearances as spontaneous display. Through observing our own body and environment, we come to recognize naturally arisen phenomena. We begin by placing a mirror at arm's length in front of us. We bathe, then dress ourselves in fine clothing and adorn ourselves with ornaments. Next, we stand in front of the mirror. We look at our reflection and praise its beauty – how lustrous its hair; how bright its eyes; how clear its complexion; how stylish its clothing, and so on. If we find ourselves feeling happy, we reproach ourselves immediately. We ask, "What am I feeling pleased for? It is my reflection that I am praising. So it should be the reflection which feels happy, not me." If we feel that the reflection is our own reflection and that praising it is the same as praising ourselves, we should remember that we, in fact, are just like another reflection – the naturally arisen display of primordial ground. We observe our surroundings; they too are mere expressions of primordial ground. These expressions have created a comprehensive, animated illusion in the mirror. From this observation, we can easily see that our mirrored image cannot know that it is a mere reflection; neither can it know that all its surrounding appearances are but illusory reflections. But, by standing outside the mirror, we are able to realize this. Relative to our mirrored reflections, we are then the enlightened ones. In a similar way, we are ignorant of ourselves being part of the natural display of primordial ground. We are not aware that the world around us is of the same illusory nature. Because of our ignorance, we are the deluded ones. Those who realize the truth are the enlightened ones.

Practicing this way, the practitioner will eventually recognize that phenomena are but the boundless vitality of the *dharmadhatu,* the great compassion of the Buddha. Like animated images naturally reflected by a mirror, phenomena spontaneously arise from the *dharmadhatu.* From this we can easily understand the aspect of display. The aspect of display is inherent in *dharmadhatu;* it spontaneously gives rise to myriad expressions, the expressions of primordial ground. The aspect of display is also intrinsic to our *rigpa,* our primordial mind. Phenomena arise naturally arise from our mind in a similar way. Standing in front of the mirror, we contemplate silently for a moment. Then, with our new insight, we again observe our reflection and the surrounding environment. We will quickly come to realize that all these appearances – the body, the world – are mere illusions to the mind.

We can also practise by criticizing the shortcomings of our reflection until we feel irritated. Then, we contemplate introspectively as above. While alternating between praising and criticizing, we observe our response carefully. Practising this way can strengthen our realization of the illusory nature of the body and its surrounding environment. If we have gained some realizations from the practice of the bardo of living, this practice will help us gain deeper insight into the aspect of display.

The second part of the daytime practice of illusory body, speech and mind is the practice of recognizing sound as natural cognizance. It is a practice of recognizing the countless expressions of sound as mere natural cognizance through listening to our own echoes. The practice of recognizing sound as natural cognizance focuses on the cognizant aspect of sound rather than on visual appearances. Of our base consciousness, the most active are our eye consciousness and ear consciousness. Hence, of our five senses – seeing, hearing, smell, taste and touch – seeing and hearing are relatively more important. Therefore, in addition to observing the illusory nature of visual appearances, like body and form, we should place equally high emphasis on recognizing the illusory nature of sound. In Buddhist terminology, sound is sometimes referred to as speech or, more technically, as wind. In future chapters, we talk about many practices of purifying our wind; they belong to the area of speech practice, and are different from the practice of recognizing the illusory nature of sound.

The practice of recognizing sound as natural cognizance requires us to go to a wide open area and yell our heart out. It does not matter what kind of sound we make; we can shout the mantra OM AH HUNG or we can shout foul language. Whether our words are virtuous, non-virtuous, elegant or vulgar is not important. Whatever we shout, we listen attentively to the echoes of the sounds. We listen objectively, without grasping the notion that these sounds are our echoes; they are mere sound vibrations. While listening, we contemplate, "What is the difference between the sound of my voice and its echo?" If we let go of our I, we will come to realize that speech and echo are mere vibrations. Inherent within them is their natural cognizance, which spontaneously gives rise to their sonic variations, allowing them to be distinguished from other vibrations. Since our *rigpa* also has this cognizant aspect, we can naturally differentiate between sounds according to their different expressions. But often, our discriminatory faculty may inadvertently give rise to our self-grasping. We grasp onto an inherently existing I, regarding certain sonic variations as being "mine" and the rest as being "others." The sound of our voice and its echo are both natural cognizance, differing only in their expressions. We can say the sound of our voice is, in fact, just another variation of an echo, much as our I and our mirrored reflection were, both being illusions expressed according to their domains of existence. By practising this way, we can realize the meaning of natural cognizance and its meaning in relation to other base consciousness such as form, smell, and touch.

The third part of the daytime practice of illusory body, speech and mind is the practice of recognizing the nature of mind as being empty. It is a practice of recognizing the illusory nature of our emotional responses, or mental actions, through observing how our mind is deceived into reacting. We can visualize ourselves as mirrored reflections, like reflections of primordial ground. We can then alternately flatter and criticize ourselves, as in the first practice. We should flatter ourselves until we feel utterly superior, and criticize ourselves until we feel totally worthless. If we have a partner with whom to practise, we can have them abruptly bang on a table without warning while we are completely absorbed in the above practice. This sudden action should give pause to our running thoughts and fix our mind right in the moment of feeling either superior or worthless. In this sudden lucid moment, we can dispel our illusory mental indulgence by contemplating the following: "Why should I feel this way? It is my mirrored reflection which is being flattered (or criticized). How illusive is my present state of mind?" If we have no partner with whom to practice, at the right moment, we can bang the table or clap our hands to wake ourselves. This "whack and holler" practice is common among Chan Buddhists, who consider it very effective in instantly placing the mind in the here and now.

I recall two memorable experiences of this sudden awakening. In 1964, Guru Qu Wenlu (1883-1973), the disciple of Gara Lama Trinley Gyatso (who is also known as Nora Rinpoche) granted me the fourth empowerment of Yamantaka. He instructed me to kneel before him and meditate on the body *mandala* of the deity and the related seed syllable. I followed his instructions and meditated on them single-pointedly. Suddenly, iridescent flashes of light swept past my eyes. Before me, I saw Guru Qu waving a crystal *vajra* sceptre. He said, "The deity you meditate on is neither the same as, nor different from, the luminous iridescence of this crystal." Instantly, I realized the meaning of natural cognizance of *rigpa*. Suddenly, Guru Qu hit the table. I felt as if I had suddenly awakened from a dream. From this instantaneous awakening, I gained deeper insight into the meaning of natural cognizance, and its immensely vibrant naturally arisen expressions.

The other unforgettable experience happened in 1984 in a meeting with my root guru, Dudjom Rinpoche. One morning, after imparting some precious instructions to me, he said, "This will be our last meeting in this lifetime." Feeling tears welling in my eyes, I knelt down and paid homage to him, imploring him to stay longer in this world. When I looked up, his rosary beads swept past my eyes, and he laughed merrily. As with Guru Qu twenty years before, I felt as if I had suddenly awakened from a dream. At the same time, I felt that the moment was like a scene projected on a television. I too burst into laughter. I paid homage and bid farewell to Guru Dudjom Rinpoche. The guru's laughter and the sweeping of his rosary beads had the same awakening effect on me as the "whack and holler" method of Guru Qu. However, a single moment of insight is not sufficient. We must practise repeatedly to attain the final realization. Following our practice of the impure illusory body, we progress to practice of the pure illusory body.

The Practice of Pure Illusory Body

The practice of pure illusory body is a practice to eradicate our clinging to ordinary appearances. It is sometimes referred to as training in pure view. The practice involves two steps. The first is a mundane approach while the second is supra-mundane. According to the authentic teachings, the first step involves the guru, dressed as Vajrasattva, sitting in the lotus posture with his disciples sitting in front of him. The disciples observe the guru through a crystal sceptre that they hold in front of themselves. Multiple iridescent reflections of Vajrasattvas shine through the sceptre. By observing this, disciples try to gain understanding that all phenomena are mere appearances, empty of inherent existence. In short, we refer to these appearances, which are in essence empty, as appearance-emptiness. In a more modern adaptation of this practice, the guru no longer dresses up to serve as the object of meditation. Instead, the disciples observe each other, or observe a photograph through a crystal sceptre or crystal ball. The essential point is for them to experience that all phenomena are but appearance-emptiness.

When we say appearances are empty of inherent existence, it is important to note here that we are describing only the nature of appearances. The other connate aspects are its natural cognizance and faculty, which exist simultaneously and inseparably. Therefore, appearance-emptiness is beyond four extremes. We cannot just say that it is non-existent, nor can we grasp it as real and insist that it truly exists. The former description leans to the extreme of the aspect of emptiness while the latter skews to the extreme of the aspects of natural cognizance and function. We cannot say that it is "both existent as well as non-existent," nor can we say that it is "neither existent nor non-existent." If we describe it that way, we are segregating its nature, natural cognizance and function as three independent, separate aspects. In fact, these three aspects are connate and cannot be separated. Through contemplating this, we will stay away from the four extremes and eventually realize the meaning of "unproduced." This is the profound perfection of wisdom stated in the *Heart Sutra*: "Form is empty; emptiness is form. Form is not other than emptiness; emptiness is not other than form."

The practice based on this supra-mundane approach, which comes from Buddha Shakyamuni himself, is of an advanced level. In order to gain benefit from this practice, we must be familiar with the generation-stage meditation practice on a deity and his or her *mandala*. Pure Land practitioners, who are not trained in such a meditation practice, can follow the sixteen-step instruction described in the *Sutra of Contemplation on Buddha Amitayus* and meditate by visualizing

Buddha Amitabha and his *mandala* together with his retinue of Avalokiteshvara and Mahasthamaprapta. This would be equivalent to Vajrayana generation-stage meditation practice.

Generally speaking, generation-stage meditation can be practised as follows. First, we visualize Buddha Amitabha or Buddha Vajradhara (or the deity of our regular practice) appearing in the space before us. We concentrate until we have a clear image in our mind. It is important that our vision of the deity and its *mandala* be luminous and vivid, and suggestive of the wisdom and compassion pervading space. If in our meditation we visualize the Buddha as a stone statue or flat picture, not only will we gain no benefit, it may actually be harmful. Next, we visualize the Buddha in the space before us melting into luminous nectar and dissolving into us through our crown, purifying all our negativities. Our body, speech and mind become the Buddha's body, speech and mind. (The most common mistake here is to close our eyes completely during meditation. It is important to keep our eyes relaxed and slightly open.) Such visualization practice is a practice of appearance-emptiness. It serves to counter our grasping of ordinary appearances. If we indeed exist inherently in this solid form, it would then be impossible for us to visualize ourselves taking on the form of a Buddha. After our formal meditation practice, we must remember to extend this mindfulness to our everyday lives, and see the world that appears before us as the pure land of the Buddha. This training in pure view is very important because it is the foundation for the practice of the bardo of dreams and for the bardo of *dharmata*. We need to practise repeatedly to realize that our lives and the world around us are actually like illusions, like dreams. When we attain such realization, we attain the supreme abiding of reality-itself (*dharmata*); and when we have some experience of the latter, we attain the supreme abiding of the mind-itself.

CHAPTER 11

Practice Instruction for the Bardo of Dreams (Part 2)

THE SECOND PRACTICE OF THE BARDO OF DREAMS is the night-time practice of dreaming. The practice consists of the following three parts:

1. Apprehending the dream state;
2. Emanation and transformation; and
3. Dispelling obstacles to dreaming.

Before discussing the practice of the bardo of dreams, we should review some of the writings on dreams by the ancient masters of the Buddhist tradition. The earliest discussion of dreams can be found in the Buddhist text *Milinda-panha* (or *The Questions of Milinda*) (100 BCE), which is considered one of the most authoritative works of its time. The text consists of dialogues: questions posed by King Milinda (also known as Menander) and answered by Nagasena. Their conversations represent a profound exposition of Buddhist doctrine on such topics as reincarnation, karma, nirvana and so forth. In addition, the text includes in-depth discussions on dreaming.

In the dialogues of *Milinda-panha*, Nagasena says, "Dreams are expressions of prophetic intuitions conceded to the locus of the heart." To the king's question of what causes the experience of dreams, Nagasena answers, "Your Majesty, there are six different kinds of people experiencing dreams. Those who have problems with internal wind circulation experience dreams; those who have problems with bile secretion experience dreams; those who have problems with phlegm experience dreams; those who are subject to the whims of gods and goddesses experience dreams; those with habitual dispositions experience dreams; and those who see prophetic visions in their dreams experience dreams. Among them, only the prophetic dreams are real dreams – all others are mere delusive expressions." In other words, although those who suffer from physical sickness (wind, bile and phlegm) and mental anguish (the influence of gods and goddesses) dream, their dreams are delusive. Only those who have the ability to manifest prophetic visions in their dream states are able to dream real dreams, to receive prophetic intuitions conceded to the locus of the heart, that is, as if received through the crown and descending to the heart chakra.

In ancient days, many considered dreams to be prognostic. The *Dream Book*, ancient Chinese folklore from the collections of the *Jade Box Tales*, offers elaborate explanations of the different prophetic interpretations of dreams. However, such explanations only equate dreams as foretelling, and do not adequately explain why people have dreams or how prophetic dreams are conceded to the locus of the heart.

Written later, the *Abhidharma-maha-vibhasa-sastra* quotes Vasumitra's comments on dreams, and explains that their occurrence is caused by five contributing factors: anxiety of the mind; habitual tendency; discriminatory awareness; reminiscence and past experiences; and foretokens (or premonitions) conferred by spirits. Under this classification, the causes of dreams are grouped according to our various states of mind. Psychic abilities, referred to as "foretokens conferred by spirits," are considered to be mere projections of our conscious awareness.

Great Buddhists of ancient times were very advanced in their thinking to have established the relationship between dreams and states of mind. According to the dream practice of the Nyingma tradition, dreams are viewed as expressions of our karmic imprints, which include all our past and present anxieties, behavioural patterns, discriminatory awareness, experiences and so forth. They are the imprints in our minds accumulated over the course of life after life. The Nyingma practices are focussed upon transcending these states of mind. Since the relationship between our dreams and our state of mind is so close, the practice of dreams has become an integral part of the path to liberation.

After gaining some fundamental understanding of dreams, we can proceed to discussion of the first night-time practice on dreaming, that of apprehending the dream state. Apprehending the dream state means that we apprehend, or know, we are dreaming while we are in our dream. Some people misunderstand this practice as an exercise to recall dreams after they have woken. That is not the real point of the practice. Many people can remember what they dreamed – there is no need for such a practice! In order for us to be able to apprehend our own dream state fully while we are dreaming, we need to practise progressively according to the stages of the path. The intent of the practice is to let us realize while in our dream state the illusory nature of our bodies, and the environment around us. When we do the practice in conjunction with the daytime practice of illusory body, it will help us realize that phenomena we see during the daytime are the same as appearances in our dreams. The way we exist in this world of phenomena is identical to the way our dream bodies appear in our dream worlds. Both worlds are illusory, differing only in their planes of existence. When we can recognize different dreamlike expressions in their different formats of existence, we have gained the realization of dreams.

Attempting to recall our dreams during our waking hours will not bring us the realization of dreams as described above. When we recollect our dreams, we are observing a dream state from a waking perspective; dreaming and waking are two different states of being. Since the subject observing and the object being observed are on different planes of existence, the practice is, in fact, contrary to those of illusory body and apprehending the dream state. In the daytime practice of illusory body, the illusory person is part of the illusory world he is observing. Similarly, in the night-time practice of apprehending the dream state, the dream body is part of the dream world he is observing. In both practices, observing and being observed exist in the same plane. For this reason, we can draw a parallel between the two practices; they complement each other.

Apprehending the Dream State

We begin the practice of apprehending the dream state by first observing daytime phenomena. We apply the daytime practice of illusory body, with which we should be very familiar by now, to our daily lives. We pay attention to the houses, streets and shops around us; we observe those people with whom we have just chatted and those with whom we have just closed a business deal. Whether daytime phenomena be objects or persons, we see them as appearances in a dream. If the situation permits, we can reinforce such mindfulness by calling out, "This is a dream; they are mere objects in my dream; I am dreaming."

When night-time comes we pray silently before going to sleep, "For the benefit of all sentient beings, I practise the illusion-like *samadhi*. Please help me realize that I am dreaming while I dream." After making this heartfelt wish, we go to sleep. We should assume the Sleeping Buddha posture by lying on our right side, with our head pointing north and our toes pointing south, supporting our right chin with our right hand and allowing the left hand to rest comfortably on the left thigh.

To help practitioners fall asleep easily while maintaining this special awareness, many styles of dream yoga practice are taught. We should use the method to which we feel most connected. The most common method adopted by Vajrayana practitioners is to visualize ourselves sleeping in our guru's lap, like babies slumbering in the loving arms of their mothers. Visualizing like this relaxes our bodies and minds, and helps us to fall asleep more quickly. If, however, our thoughts keep churning in our minds and refuse to settle, instead of forcing ourselves to sleep, we should turn our focus on the mental scene that most disturbs us. Much as we would use a magnifying glass to condense the sun's rays into a single point, we collect our wandering thoughts into one. This method is very helpful in inducing sleep for those with a busy mind.

Even when we have managed to relax and have had a good night's sleep, however, we may not have the faintest idea whether we have dreamed or not when we wake up. We shouldn't be alarmed – it is a very common problem. We need to be patient and repeat over and over the daytime practice of illusory body and the night-time practice of apprehending the dream state. Before sleeping, we should continue to make a heartfelt prayer to the enlightened ones to help us apprehend our dream state for the sake of all sentient beings. If we practise sincerely this way, we should be able to apprehend our dream state in seven days unless we are stressed. If we have worries, grievances or unfulfilled longings that prevent us from falling asleep, or if we have been having vague, unclear dreams that we cannot recall in the morning (not to mention, apprehend during sleep), then, as we fall asleep, we should do a special visualization. We should visualize at our throat a beautiful red lotus with four delicate petals as smooth as silk, on the surface of which lie tiny droplets of morning dew. The lotus has a sweet, enticing scent, At its centre is a luminous drop the size of a pea, deep red in colour, sparkling like a ruby. Through praying to the enlightened ones and visualizing the lotus, we should soon be able to apprehend our dream state.

Another common problem is to wake up at the very moment we have apprehended our dream state. We shouldn't be discouraged; we should just go back to sleep. Sometimes, the same dream repeats itself, while at other times it even carries on from where it left off. When these things happen, our practice will become easier. Very soon, we will be fully aware of our dream state while we are dreaming.

Emanation and Transformation

The second part of the night-time practice on dreaming is the practice of dream emanation and transformation. Since dreams are emanations of habitual disposition or karmic imprints, we can purify our habitual disposition through transforming our dreams. This is the purpose of the practice of emanation and transformation.

Success in transforming our dreams depends largely on our awareness of our dream state while we are dreaming, and it is not easy to do. Those who are familiar with the Vajrayana generation-stage deity meditation have an advantage over others in this particular area of practice. When we are experienced in visualizing ourselves in the form of a deity during or after meditation, we can apply the same technique to transform our dreams. While we are dreaming, we can generate ourselves as a deity and transform the environment around us into the deity's *mandala*. Without such training, the practice of emanation and transformation may take more time to master.

Besides helping us to transform our dreams, the daily practice of deity meditation can also remove unnecessary fear when we encounter nightmares. For example, if in a dream, we see an uncontrollable forest fire racing towards us, we may protect ourselves by generating as a deity. Having transformed into a higher being, we automatically feel secure and protected. Our fears instantly subside. Some practitioners practise transforming their dreams with miraculous powers. Actions such as transforming a blazing fire into a cool, placid lake, transforming a murderer's knife into a leaf of the wish-fulfilling tree, or transforming a *mara* into a holy being are advanced-level practices of emanation and transformation. I personally do not like engaging in this kind of practice, because the goal of my Dharma practice is not miraculous power. For this reason, I do not place emphasis upon it in my dreams.

I recall a memorable occurrence of transforming a dream. I dreamed of my grandmother, and, because she had died in a fire, her entire body was charred. Instantly, I was aware that I was dreaming, and immediately transformed my dream according to the practice of transforming dreams. I generated a seed syllable, from which a thousand-petal lotus arose to cradle her. After that, I woke up. This is an example of what we can easily achieve when we are familiar with generation-stage meditation practices. There is no need to generate miraculous powers in our dreams.

It is not always necessary to generate oneself as a deity in order to transform appearances in a dream. As long as we recognize that we are dreaming, we can transform our dreams. For example, imagine that we dream of a huge tidal wave rolling towards us to sweep us away. Instead of panicking, we think: "It is only a dream, and I am only a dream body. Nothing can really be swept away by these waters." We jump fearlessly into the rolling waves without hesitation. Instantly, our dream is transformed. Alternatively, we can think, "I am only dreaming. This tidal wave is just another scary illusion in a dream. It cannot really carry me away or cause any real damage." Again our dream is transformed. Sometimes in the dream the water will continue to pour down upon us, but without harming us; other times, it may transform into a peaceful meadow. No matter what kind of transformation takes place, the choice we make in the dream will not prove harmful.

Before engaging in the practice of transformation in our dreams, we can add a preliminary exercise to prepare our minds. The purpose is to make use of the in-between sleep state to familiarize ourselves with the mental action of transformation. For example, just before we doze off, we can try to transform the shadowy images of our environment into a large cradle or a comfortable bed covered with rose petals. If we can change our thoughts in this in-between sleep state, transforming our dreams is just an easy step away. Although helpful, this preliminary practice is not recommended for people who have a history of insomnia. If we have difficulty falling asleep, to ease ourselves into sleep we should try the practice mentioned earlier, that of visualizing at our throat a red four-petal lotus with a tiny luminous red drop at its centre. The key to this practice is to focus all our senses, especially our wandering thoughts, on the luminous red drop. We concentrate and do not let our focus waver for the slightest split-second.

What should we do if our thoughts keep wandering even when we try hard to keep our focus? We should not worry. When discursive thoughts arise, we should immediately dissolve them into the luminous red drop in the centre of the lotus. For example, while we are trying to focus our mind, a disturbing thought of someone who has been urging us to close a deal, arises. No matter how urgent this matter is, we do not let it overwhelm us. Instead, we expand the red drop at the centre of the lotus to envelop that person, like a flower capturing its insect prey. We let him dissolve into it and then we transform the drop into a red ruby. It is always better to control our thoughts when they first arise. If we allow them to wander randomly, out of control, insomnia is certain. To increase the power of our mind so that it can control our thoughts, we need to visualize o a red drop, which is like a command centre, at the centre of our throat. If we fall asleep easily, and are even able to transform our dreams at will, we will definitely enjoy many sweet dreams.

The Four Dispersals

There are four major obstacles that practitioners commonly encounter in the practices of apprehending the dream state and of emanation and transformation.

These obstacles are:

1.   Dispersal through waking;
2.   Dispersal through forgetfulness;
3.   Dispersal through confusion; and
4.   Dispersal through emptiness.

Dispersal through waking means that we wake up the moment we apprehend our dream state. There are two necessary criteria. First, we apprehend the dream state, and second, we wake up immediately and remember our dreams. If we have only a vague memory of what we have dreamed, or if we cannot remember our dreams at all, then we cannot be considered to have apprehended our dream state, and hence we have not yet encountered the problem of dispersal through waking. Guru Padmasambhava taught us a method to remedy this problem. Before we sleep, we visualize a luminous, dark blue drop the size of a pea, called the black syllable, at the centre of each of our feet. We focus our mind on these two black syllables. The key is to visualize them in a dark blue colour, so dark that they look almost black. Although dark blue, the syllables are luminous, crystal-clear and sparkling. To visualize glittering dark light plays with your mind! Whenever I visualized these blue-black syllables at the centre of my feet, I felt dark blue light rushing from the centre of my feet to my heart chakra. I was so relaxed that it seemed I was submerged in a deep blue sea. I fell asleep very quickly. However, that did not guarantee any apprehended dreams. After persevering with the practice for nine months, I finally had a dream, and I was also able to transform the scene in my dream. We all need patience and effort to succeed in our practice. When an obstacle arises, we must try to remedy it immediately. We just keep trying, again and again, even when we do not have any apprehended dreams. We must not become impatient and discouraged; we must have faith in the practice. One day, we will discover its magic.

Dispersal through forgetfulness is another obstacle to this practice. It is so called because our dreamscapes become fuzzy the moment we apprehend our dream state. As if drugged, we have a vague sense that we are in a dream but cannot follow or remember the scenes. Our dream-minds keep roaming around, like the wild thoughts that whirl through our minds when we first learn to meditate. In both cases, they are the reflections of our restless, wandering minds. Yet, when we are fully awake, we can let our minds roam around – we can muse about vacations or daydream about our loved one. We can let our minds wander without ever worrying that our thoughts will become fuzzy. Our dream awareness, however, behaves differently. If we let it drift, instantly our dreams will become blurred. We can remedy this problem through doing more practice of illusory body in the daytime. As described earlier, we practise seeing all daytime phenomena as appearances in a dream, and let our mind explore its landscape. We practise diligently and pray wholeheartedly, "May I apprehend my dream state and not get confused." Perseverance and faith can strengthen our minds and help us make leaps in our progress.

The third obstacle we often encounter is dispersal through confusion. Dreams that are caused mainly by habitual disposition are prone to haziness. Those who have lucid dreams have purer, lighter karmic imprints, while those who frequently have fuzzy dreams have deeper negative habitual disposition. For example, if we repeatedly dream of helping, whether it involves saving an ant or being rescued by others, we must have a strong habitual disposition of helping. The habitual disposition of helping can be expressed very differently in our daily life. It may develop into a positive trait of being helpful or a negative habit of constantly relying on the help of others. Because habitual disposition can be expressed either positively or negatively, we can counter the obstacle of dispersal through confusion by changing our habits. In general, the more negatively our habitual disposition is developed (e.g. when helping is expressed negatively in the form of helping where help is not welcome), the fuzzier our dreams will become. The more positive it is cultivated (e.g. when helping is expressed positively in the form of volunteer work to help the poor), the more lucid our dreams will appear. Hence, to remedy the problem of dispersal through confusion, we need to change our bad habits and cultivate a more positive attitude to life in general.

Because negative habitual disposition is the main cause of dispersal through confusion, the practitioner of the Tibetan Buddhist tradition will try to surmount this obstacle through practices of purification, confession and requesting Buddha to bestow blessings. These practices are intended to cultivate more positive attitudes and lead us away from such obstacles. For example, when we request Buddha to bestow blessings, we might sincerely wish for a stable job so that we have the resources to practise dharma, and to help others in the same way. In this way, our positive propensities will naturally increase.

The last of the four obstacles is dispersal through emptiness. This happens when we yearn avidly for dreams or when we just cannot fall asleep. Both cases initiate a spiraling effect, dispersing our mindfulness and preventing focus. In the first case, we seem to have fallen asleep but, in fact, we have not. We experience fleeting phases of scattered thoughts which we cannot remember. In the second case, we are sleepless and have not yet arrived at the dream state. That is different from experiencing no dreams, which is the result of deep sleep. Guru Padmasambhava taught a method to counter this problem. We should focus our mind on a luminous, dark blue drop at our heart. The drop resembles the one discussed earlier in remedying the problem of dispersal through waking. It is crystal clear, dark blue in colour, and radiant. Concentrating our mind on the drop instead of eagerly yearning for dreams, can ease us into sleep much more quickly. However, whether we can apprehend our dream state and transform our dreams after we have fallen asleep is a different matter.

The above visualization of a dark blue drop at the heart is slightly different from the one mentioned earlier, that of visualizing a four-petal red lotus at the throat. Concentrating the mind on a red drop is more suitable for those of us who are weak or easily feel cold. If our body is strong and easily becomes hot, then visualizing a dark blue drop is more beneficial. The average person can try either method.

In the Nyingma tradition, the bardo of dreams practice is considered very important. A great deal of emphasis is placed on this practice because if we do not master it well, we cannot progress to the next two practices – the bardo of *dharmata* and the bardo of existence – which are the most important practices upon the moment of our death. In other words, if we have not mastered this practice, we will not be able to control our own rebirth. Many who do the practices of liberation through the six bardos consider the success of the practice of the bardo of dreams pivotal to liberation. However, the more anxious we are, the more difficult our practice will become. We must not let attainment itself become our obstacle. We should relax and relish our practice. If we gain insight into the illusory nature of the world of phenomena, if we always see ourselves and the world around us as scenes on television, and if we maintain a balance between concentration and relaxation to perfect the daytime practice of illusory body and the night-time practice of dreaming, then eventually, we will apprehend our dream state. A balanced state of mind is the real key to the success of the two practices.

CHAPTER 12

Practice Instruction for the Bardo of Dreams (Part 3)

T HE PRACTICE OF THE FOUR CLEAR LIGHTS is the third and concluding part of the practice instruction for the bardo of dreams, and is in effect the core of the entire practice. In this chapter we will briefly explain the practice and its related principles. We need not go into great detail because the actual practice needs to be personalized and fine-tuned regularly according to the practitioner's personal experience. Because the instructions are so carefully tailored, what benefits one practitioner may not benefit another. When engaging in the actual practice, it is important that we seek our guru's advice.

The practices of the four clear lights are:

1. Clear light of awareness;
2. Clear light of element;
3. Clear light of guru; and
4. Clear light of *bindu* (drop).

Attaining one or more of the four clear lights is, however, not the goal of the concluding practice of clear light, but merely a tool to help us reach the objective, which is to realize the clear light of purity. The practices of the four clear lights are thus methods to induce the clear light of purity.

What is the Clear Light of Purity?

The clear light of primordial purity can only be induced; it cannot arise through the effort of meditation. No matter how slight, there is always a certain degree of contrivance inherent within the act of meditation. While there are mental fabrications, our minds are inevitably subject to dualistic concepts. Holy versus mundane, virtuous versus non-virtuous, produced versus non-produced, samsara versus nirvana, and even light versus darkness are all dualistic concepts fabricated in our dichotomized world. Upon this impure ground, the clear light of purity will not manifest. It is called the clear light of purity because it is a state of immaculate purity, free from all dualistic concepts and free of elaboration.

Although the clear light of purity will not arise from the effort of meditation, it can be induced through the four clear lights attained from intentional meditation practice. Although such a mind of clear light is not completely free of dualistic impressions, it can induce the arising of the clear light of purity that is immaculately pure, completely free of dualistic traces, and beyond words and concepts. Because the clear light of purity is free from all traces of contrivance, it is said to be primordially pure.

The process of inducing the clear light of purity requires a skilful balance between effort and non-effort, action and non-action. If we are too eager to "induce" the resultant state, it becomes just another deliberate act. Such deliberation is not instrumental in inducing the clear light of purity. This resultant state is tricky to attain. The challenge we have to overcome is to realize a state that is free from all dualistic traces, a state that transcends time and space, while we are effectively bound by those constraints.

Realization of the clear light of purity is a major part of liberation. However, that alone is not complete liberation in itself. If we become too eager for the challenge to complete the attainment, once again we fall into the trap of our grasping minds – and then the previously realized state is no longer "pure." On the other hand, if we do not put deliberate effort into our practice, how can we know if our attainment is firmly grounded? It is quite a conundrum.

In some traditions, the realization of clear light of purity is considered the final attainment. They consider the existence of clear light as the emanation of Thusness, and define it as the realization of the "accomplished nature" (Skt. *paripanna-svabhava*). This is the view of the Shentong (Tib. *gzhan stong*) school which basically says the nature of mind is "empty of other" but not of itself. The Nyingma Tradition does not share the view of the Shentong School. According to our tradition, the realization of innate clear light of purity is not the ultimate goal. In order to attain the ultimate realization, the practitioner must continue practising until she realizes the threefold natural liberations.

By now, we should have a general understanding of the clear light of purity. We should be aware that the labelling of certain states as pure is only a means of communication that allows us to understand in a way our conceptual minds can comprehend. We need to be aware that even a concept such as purity is dualistic: it comes into existence only when there is an opposing concept of impurity. Although we need labels and concepts to function in our domain of time and space, the ultimate state of liberation is beyond these constraints. When we try to understand concepts such as purity or mind we should see them as references only. We must be very careful not to grasp them in our worldly way. This is the meaning behind the "three statements" explained in the *Diamond Sutra*. A is not A; we name it as A. Clear light of purity is not clear light of purity; we name it as clear light of purity (when, in truth, it is neither pure nor impure; it is the state of purity). We can now proceed to discussing the topic of being induced.

The clear light of purity can be induced because it is inherent within us. Not only do we have this innate purity, the entire *dharmadhatu* is also pervaded by this intrinsic purity. We cannot see the clear light of purity in the *dharmadhatu,* however, when such a clear light is not manifested within us. As with a blind person when his optical nerve is damaged, the luminosity of eye sense does not manifest, and his eye consciousness is unable to perceive visual images. Hence, he is unable to realize light in the world of phenomena.

The purpose of meditation on the four clear lights is to induce our innate clear light of purity (sometimes referred to as intrinsic luminosity). In theory, when this innate luminosity is manifested from within us, we can then perceive the clear light of purity of *dharmadhatu.* Why do we say in theory? Even when we have realized our innate clear light of purity, we are not yet able to apprehend the true expression of the clear light of purity of *dharmadhatu.* This true expression is obscured by the light of impurity of our domain of time and space. It is as if we are trapped in a completely enclosed room of darkness that has never seen a ray of light; we do not even know what light means. We have become so accustomed to living in darkness that we think it is normal. We call this delusion or ignorance.

As stated above, the realization of our innate clear light of purity is not the final goal of the concluding practice of clear light. From that realization onward, we need to continue with our practice to realize the clear light of *dharmadhatu.* When have attained both realizations, we can be considered to have realized the clear light of purity – the goal of the concluding practice of clear light. We practise the four clear lights because they can serve as catalysts to induce the clear light of purity. They provide the conditions under which the clear light of purity of *dharmadhatu* can manifest itself. When our innate clear light of purity is induced naturally while we are travelling the four practice pathways, from there on, the clear light of purity of the *dharmadhatu* will eventually manifest itself and be realized.

Under which four conditions may the clear light of purity of *dharmadhatu* arise?

Clear Light of Sleep

The clear light of purity of the *dharmadhatu* manifests itself during our deepest sleep. However, we cannot know whether we have realized our innate clear light of purity. As mentioned earlier, a person who lives in darkness does not know what light is. Within the practices of the four clear lights, the attainment of the clear light of awareness can be compared to a dark room being lit. First, we light a flame to let the people inside the room know there is something called light. This first experience of light grants them the chance to perceive sunlight some day. The clear light of awareness can induce our innate clear light of purity to arise spontaneously. With such experience, we can eventually realize the clear light of sleep.

Clear Light of Death

The second is the clear light we experience at the time of our death. It manifests at two instances when we die (this is discussed in the chapter on the bardo of dying). Those who have not practised the path, however, will not be able to see the clear light of death. Even if they can see it, all they will experience is a flash of radiant light. They might be startled, but they will not be able to retain that experience and turn it into a realization. When a person can retain the experience and turn it into a realization, he has attained liberation. The practice of the clear light of elements can induce our innate clear light of purity and enable us to realize the clear light of death of the *dharmadhatu* upon our death. The clear light of death cannot be realized during our lifetime, but only upon the moment of death. Unlike the clear light of sleep, the true expression of which can be realized through our innate clear light of purity, the experience of the clear light of death, can only serve as a reference, like a dark room being lit for the first time.

Clear Light of Guru and Clear Light of *Bindu*

The third and fourth lights are the clear light of guru and the clear light of *bindu* (drop). Unlike the clear light of sleep and clear light of death, which arise naturally, the clear light of guru and clear light of *bindu* can be brought about by force of meditation.

What approach can we take to induce the clear light of purity of *dharmadhatu* to arise without mental deliberation? We mentioned earlier that once there is mental deliberation, our minds are considered impure, and the clear light of purity will not arise. We can eliminate the element of mental deliberation by dividing the practice into two parts according to its two aspects – its perceiving and perceived aspects. We do not aim to realize the clear light of purity of *dharmadhatu* directly through the practice. The approach here is first to realize each individual aspect – and we can do that with deliberate effort. When our attainments are integrated, the clear light of purity of *dharmadhatu* will spontaneously arise. Using this method, we can realize the clear light of purity of *dharmadhatu* with a mind that is free of deliberation or contrivance.

We can say that the goal of the practice of clear light of guru is a practice of recognizing the perceiving aspect of the clear light of purity of *dharmadhatu* while the practice of the clear light of *bindu* focuses on recognizing its perceived aspect. The practitioner needs to complete these two practices before the clear light of purity of *dharmadhatu* can be spontaneously attained. The perceiving and perceived aspects are terms commonly used by the Yogacara School. They correspond with the Nyingma view that both of these aspects can arise through our reflexive awareness. When both aspects are realized, a new state will naturally arise. The perceived aspect is analogous to mirror images, while the perceiving aspect is akin to the mirror's inherent capability. When the mirror is fully equipped with the capability of manifesting images, and images can be reflected on its surface, then reflections are deemed to arise. When the two conditions are met, there is no doubt that we can perceive the combined effect – effortlessly mirrored reflections.

The practice of the clear light of guru is intended to realize the aspect of manifestation of the clear light of purity of *dharmadhatu* – that is to realize its inherent capability to generate the state of the clear light of purity, which is analogous to realizing the inherent capability of a mirror to generate reflections. On the other hand, the practice of the clear light of *bindu* is intended to realize the aspect of expression of the clear light of purity of *dharmadhatu* – that is to realize its form is comparable to reflections on the mirror. Once our realizations of both aspects are integrated effortlessly, we can spontaneously, and without any contrivance, realize the state of the clear light of purity of *dharmadhatu*.

We must note that there is a huge difference between an appearance and a realized state. Appearance is an image that is not alive. However, a realized state is endowed with many living qualities. We might say it has extra dimensions. When an immigration officer tries to match a passport photograph to the traveller in front of him, he sees no more in the photo than the person's physical appearance. But when the traveller's family members view the same photograph, the very same image seems to possess life. They immediately recognize the traveler as a living person. "He must have been very tense when this picture was taken," they might say. "His smile is so unnatural. What was he thinking, putting on this stern look? Was he worried about not getting his passport?" All these vivid details appear to the minds of the family members but not to that of the immigration officer. This is the difference between a mere form of appearance and a realized state. From this example, we can easily see that a state has more dimensions.

It is important to stress the above point to clarify that the realization of the clear light of purity is not about realizing its form, but its state. That is why, in addition to realizing its perceived aspect, we must also realize its perceiving aspect. When they are combined, a new state will arise. This state can be spontaneously realized.

I would like to expand a little on the words used to describe the two aspects: the perceiving and perceived aspects. Some Nyingma scholars consider the above terminology too general to bring out their intrinsic meanings. They prefer to use the terms natural cognizance and infinite display for a more accurate definition. We already explained these two terms when we discussed the primordial ground in previous chapters. The differences between these terms are subtle: one, the perceived aspect refers only to mirrored images whereas cognizance further points out the differentiable quality inherent in the mirrored images; and two, the perceiving aspect refers only to the inherent capability of the mirror to reflect whereas infinite display further points out that the capability is the boundless vitality of the *dharmadhatu*. In this chapter, we use the more general version of these terms. The more technical terms of natural cognizance and infinite display, which have been previously discussed, are used in later chapters when the situation requires.

The Practice Instruction on Attaining the Mind of Clear Light – The Clear Light of Awareness

To practice the clear light of awareness, we should engage ourselves in a formal retreat for at least one month. During the retreat, we need to set boundaries to limit the activities of our body, speech and mind. We should eat lightly and stay within the area of our retreat. On the 15th of each month, we should practice guru yoga and meditation on our personal deity and dharma protector. These guidelines are set because we must stay extremely focused and mindful in our practices; otherwise, the clear light of sleep will not arise and realization will be difficult to attain.

The actual practice of clear light of sleep is very simple. Before we fall asleep, we place ourselves in the Sleeping Buddha posture, focusing on a white luminous drop, the size of a pea, at the centre of our heart. We visualize the drop radiating brilliant white light, pervading our body and mind. We try to fall asleep in the luminosity that we are contemplating. When we gain familiarity with the practice, the clear light of sleep will arise like a dream. It is vast and clear, like a cloudless sky. This is the realization of our innate clear light of purity. Since this clear light arises from the mind-itself, we need to continue our practice to make further advancement. When we advance to the next stage, we practise falling asleep in the non-dual state of luminous emptiness, in which there is no longer a need to place our mind at our heart. In the practice, we are to realize the clear light of purity of *dharmadhatu* in our deep sleep. Since we have not yet discussed the non-dual state of luminous emptiness, we will not go into detail about the practice in this chapter.

The practice of the clear light of death is derived from the manner of our death. When we die, our five elements – earth, water, fire, wind, consciousness – dissolve in successive stages. In the first stage, as our earth element dissolves into the water element, our limbs and body stiffen. In the second stage, as our water element dissolves into the fire element, our mouth and tongue become very dry. In the third stage, as our fire element dissolves into the wind element, our bodies become cold. In the final stage, as our wind element dissolves into our consciousness, our breathing stops. These are the signs of death. In the next chapter, we discuss how to make use of these signs to attain liberation upon death. In this chapter, we focus on how our sleep resembles the process of death.

When we fall asleep, our physical activities diminish and our bodies become relaxed. Our forehead is warm even when the room temperature is low. This is the stage when the earth element dissolves into the water element. Next, our mental activities slow down, and our body temperature maintains a certain level. This is the stage when the water element dissolves into fire element. At this stage, we seem to have fallen asleep, but our consciousness is not fully at rest. We can easily be wakened by a slight sound or any minor changes to our sense perceptions. This is the stage when the fire element dissolves into the wind element. Finally, we fall into a deep sleep. Our consciousness is fully at rest and our senses of sight, hearing, smell, taste and touch have become inactive. This is the stage when the wind element dissolves into the consciousness.

These four stages of sleep resemble the four signs we experience upon death. Hence we can make use of these experiences in hypothesizing death to realize the clear light of death. The key is to maintain the experience of luminous emptiness when these four stages arise. The awareness of luminous emptiness should have already been realized in the previous practice of the bardo of living, although it is not necessary to have realized the non-dual state of luminous emptiness. However, if we have not gained sufficient experience in the practice of the bardo of living and the daytime practice of the illusory body of the bardo of dreams, we will lack the foundation required to hypothesize the stages of death during the process of sleep.

In the practice of the clear light of guru, we visualize a luminous drop at the centre of the four-petalled lotus at our heart, which then transforms into our root guru (whose nature is no different to that of Guru Padmasambhlava). According to its outer meaning, we will receive tremendous blessings from our root guru. In its inner meaning, the light manifested by our root guru will pervade our body and mind so that we can fall asleep in its luminosity. From its secret meaning, the clear light of guru is a state beyond thought, free of elaboration. When our mind focuses on guru, we can naturally abide in the state of luminous emptiness – the state of clear light of purity of *dharmadhatu*.

The practice also has a very secret meaning which points us towards a new dimension of vitality. The mere realization of the clear light of purity without vitality is flat and incomplete. However, this flatness can be enlivened by visualization of the guru at our heart. When our root guru abides in the state of luminous emptiness at the centre of our heart, our mind will be naturally infused with his boundless vitality. When the clear light of purity is induced through our realization of the clear light of guru, we can witness ourselves and our environment existing in a state of luminous clarity. We may see ourselves lying on our bed, and also see the entire surrounding environment as if we were watching a vivid movie. This is the infinite display of the clear light of purity.

The practice of the clear light of *bindu* is a practice that follows the clear light of guru. Practitioners with superior faculties will realize the aspect of expression of the clear light of purity at the same time they realize its aspect of infinite display. In that case, they have completed the practice. However, practitioners with less sharp faculties will not be able to realize the two aspects simultaneously. Although they have realized the aspect of infinite display as in a dream, they cannot realize the clear light of purity of *dharmadhatu* because they are not yet able to form such a union. At this stage, practitioners need to practise the clear light of *bindu* in order to complete the practice.

The key to the practice of the clear light of *bindu* is to visualize countless luminous drops, the size of sesame seeds, floating in our central channel – from our crown chakra to our navel chakra – sparkling with energy and vitality. At our heart, there is a luminous red drop, slightly bigger in size. These luminous drops themselves are not equivalent to the clear light of purity; however, they are signs of its expressions. When we can realize these two aspects, the clear light of purity will definitely arise.

The above discussion has covered some key points which are normally transmitted only verbally. However, what we have discussed are only theories. When we actually engage in the practice, we need to follow our guru's personal advice and practise according to his spoken instructions; we need to practise the four clear lights alternately; and we need to discuss our practice experience with our guru frequently, and request his precious wisdom. Following this, we should realize the union of our innate clear light of purity and the clear light of purity of *dharmadhatu*.

If we cannot attain this realization after practising for some time, we can switch to the practice of the clear light of death and return to this practice later. We will certainly be able to attain liberation in the moment we enter in our bardo state. If we have no guru to consult, we can simply try to understand the theory of the four clear lights. Through the mere act of understanding, we can accumulate a vast amount of merit.

CHAPTER 13

Threefold Space and the Four Liberations – The Bardo of Meditation

THE THIRD BARDO TEACHING is the bardo of meditation, known as natural liberation of awareness. The experience of natural liberation of awareness has been likened to someone looking at his reflection in a mirror. This analogy makes natural awareness sound simple, and easy to accomplish, but it is not. The practice, which has two parts, being threefold space and the four liberations, is very advanced, and difficult to realize. Not only that, but the underlying views are difficult to grasp.

To begin, we will examine the very basic concept of awareness. The term awareness can be described as intrinsic luminous awareness. It is sometimes alternatively translated as intrinsic awareness, naked awareness or primordial awareness. In Tibetan, this exalted state is called *rigpa*. Realizing awareness is not a conceptual activity; we should not pursue awareness as if it were something tangible to be attained outside our mind. Rather, realizing awareness means experiencing our own intrinsic awareness – *rigpa*, the clear light of primordial purity. This clear light of primordial purity is not an objective phenomenon; it is not something we perceive. Because it lacks substantive existence, its nature is empty. It is a state of inner realization.

Recognizing *rigpa* involves the realization of its aspects: the clear light of purity and its primordial nature. In this chapter, we refer to this awareness by its full name, the clear light of primordial purity, to remind the reader of the aspects that constitute *rigpa*. Approached from another perspective, realizing the clear light of primordial purity is a means to realizing emptiness. As discussed earlier, we can only discern the nature of a phenomenon from its appearance and its inherent capabilities. In earlier examples, we illustrated that the way we arrive at an understanding of the nature of water is not from the water itself, but from its fluidity, its capability to clean, and other qualities. Following the same rationale, we cannot realize the nature of emptiness from emptiness itself, but rather through realizing its two aspects – its cognizance and inherent capabilities – all summarized in one term: the clear light of primordial purity. In this way, the clear light of purity is the aspect of cognizance of emptiness (or, in terms of the world of phenomena, its expression), while its being primordially abiding since beginningless time is the aspect of infinite displays of emptiness. As it is now and has been since the beginning of time, it is infused with boundless vitality, pervading space. This is the inherent capability of emptiness.

The clear light of primordial purity is a state of inner realization of emptiness. This spontaneous state is the wisdom of *tathagatagarbha*, which is often referred to in short as simply *tathgatagarbha*. When this state manifests effortlessly from the mind-itself, our mind of ignorance is transformed into the perfect state of wisdom. Meditation on threefold space is a practice to self-realize the clear light of primordial purity. Such attainment obtained through the effort of meditation, however, is not equivalent to full enlightenment. In order to attain Buddhahood, we have to rely on the guru to provide instructions for completing the path of the four liberations. When giving instructions directly to us, the guru will only indicate the general direction we should take. He points to the way to go. No detailed instructions on practice are given because at this point the path is beyond words; conceptual instructions would only be a barrier to our advancement. Because conceptual instructions cannot be provided, the analogy of a person looking at his reflection in a mirror is only a guide, a pointer to the direction of final enlightenment.

We are born into a delusive world, trapped by our own discriminatory awareness, dichotomizing all that appears to us. But before we can transcend such dualistic conceptualization, we have to use it as the basis of our practice. Take the analogy of the person looking at his reflection as an example. The mirror's reflection is just like our illusory, dualistic world. When a person looks into the mirror at his reflection, he uses the mirror's illusory image to see what his original face looks like. This looking at the original face nakedly symbolizes the realization of intrinsic awareness. By using the reflection as the basis of our observation, we can transcend what appears to be illusory. Although we must base our meditation practice on dualistic concepts, we can similarly transcend them. We transcend phenomena by being part of the phenomena. Similarly, we transcend our mind-itself by abiding in the mind-itself. When we transcend it, we instantly have a fresh experience of *rigpa*. This is the principle of liberation of awareness.

Possessing a thorough understanding of this principle is a prerequisite to the following meditation on threefold space.

Threefold Space Meditation

Of what is threefold space composed? It comprises external space, internal space and secret space. The external space refers to the physical, empty space external to us. The internal space refers to the empty channels within us that connect our heart chakra and eye chakra. The secret space is the empty *kati* channel located at the centre of our heart. The practice of threefold space meditation focuses mainly on these interconnected spaces. First, we direct our intrinsic awareness from the secret space at our heart to the internal space to our eyes. Then, we direct it to the external empty space in front of us and gaze at it single-pointedly. When we direct our awareness from the mind at our heart towards our eyes, the clear light of primordial purity manifests. When we direct awareness from our eyes to the external space, primordial wisdom naturally arises.

The practice sounds simple, but it is often done incorrectly. Firstly, gazing at external space is not the same as gazing at the sky. When we look at the sky, it feels as if we are gazing at one section of a vast, blue canopy far away. But this is not what we mean by external space. External space encompasses the space around us. Visually, we can think of the sky as being two-dimensional, whereas external space is three-dimensional. By way of analogy, we can imagine ourselves as a ladybird inside a big balloon. The inner surface of the balloon is like the sky, while the space within the balloon is external space.

If we are not aware of this difference between two-dimensional and three-dimensional space, and just stare at the sky, then we cannot claim to be meditating on the threefold space. If we do the meditation properly, our *kati* channel should appear as a tiny hollow crystal, and the channels that connect the *kati* channel to the eyes should appear as thin hollow strands. However, if we mistakenly use the two-dimensional canopy of sky as our object of gazing, our focus will be misdirected to a section of that canopy. A section of sky cannot be considered empty. If we have not properly visualized external space as being empty, it follows that our meditation on internal space and secret space will also not be empty. The key to the threefold space meditation is the meaning of empty space. It is mostly transmitted verbally, rarely in writing. Even when we possess a clear intellectual understanding of what empty space means, we should not take threefold space meditation as our beginning practice. We must first be well grounded in the practices of the bardo of living and the bardo of dreams. Frequent practice of these two bardos helps us to abide in the mind-itself. Armed with such realization, we can progress to the practice of threefold space meditation to attain natural liberation of the mind-itself.

For practitioners of superior ability who have attained liberation of the mind-itself by practising the above two bardos and can abide in the *dharmata*, the three-fold space meditation can help them complete the practice of attaining natural liberation of *dharmata*.

In the chapter on the four clear lights, we discussed how the clear light of purity can be evoked to arise effortlessly. In this chapter, we focus on realizing the primordial aspect of the clear light of purity. Merely realizing the aspect of clear light is not sufficient; we must also realize its primordial aspect before we can deem ourselves on the path of liberation. If we cannot abide in the mind-itself to such an extent that the clear light of purity can effortlessly arise, then meditation practice on threefold space will only be a waste of time. Worse, if we are not well grounded in the above-mentioned foundation practices, and zealously engage in meditating on the sky, emotional disturbance may result. After we have practised incorrectly for a prolonged period of time, reckless behaviour, depression and other problems may occur. We should be careful with our practice and take care not to advance before we are ready to do so.

Meditation on threefold space is not a rigid practice, set in stone. In reality, it is a non-referential (Tib. *dmig med*) meditation in which no object of focus can be conceptualized. In fact, we should not strive to visualize the external, internal or secret space; once we have realized the clear light of purity, threefold space is established without any effort on our part. When we meditate on threefold space properly, the clear light of purity will effortlessly arise. What we need to realize in the next step is its primordial presence.

If realized through conscious endeavour, the clear light of purity will be neither stable nor primordial, no matter how quickly it arises. The primordial clear light of purity does not need to arise because it is primordially present. It is there, just as it has always been. Under the veil of our deluded consciousness, we simply cannot recognize it. Strictly speaking, the realization of threefold space is spontaneous and effortless. At this stage, the roles of practice and meditation, concepts and theories, become insignificant. Even concepts of emptiness, cognizance and expression can all be dispensed with.

Moheyan and the Tibetans

When Buddhism first began to spread to Tibet, masters from both India and China tirelessly travelled there to spread Buddha's teachings. Among them was Moheyan, the renowned Chan Master of the Northern School. He preached that meditation should be without conceptual thoughts (thought-free), without seeking or waiting, and without analyzing or discriminating. Although a profound method, it did not escape scrutiny. When the Indian monk Kamalashila entered Tibet, he criticized Moheyan's method of meditation, and the famous debate of Samye (Tib. *bSam yas*) commenced. The outcome of the debate is not clear: according to the Dunhuang manuscripts, Moheyan was unbeaten; however, according to Tibetan records, he was convincingly defeated. Moheyan was later expelled from Tibet and banned from disseminating Buddhist teachings. Although we cannot know which historical source is more reliable, we can investigate the issues surrounding Moheyan's controversial practice.

When we study the ancient Dunhuang manuscripts from the 10th century, we find evidence suggesting that the type of meditation taught by Moheyan may not have been as simple as was recorded by the Tibetans. Among the Dunhuang manuscripts, the *Torch of the Eye of Meditation* (Tib. *bSam gtan mig gron*), written by the Nyingma Master Nubchen Sanggye Yeshe (Tib. *gNub chen Sangs rgya ye shes*), records organized teachings on the subject of thought-free meditation under the Simultaneous or Sudden (Tib. *cig car ba*) tradition. It is very possible that these teachings were received from Moheyan. They are considered advanced instructions that have a deeper meaning than being merely thought-free on an intellectual level. Such teachings are easily misunderstood and are not intended for everyone. Although we cannot go back in time to solve the mystery of this controversy, the story shows how the non-referential meditation on threefold space can easily be misunderstood. When we try to meditate as if we are not meditating, we are already working towards a contrived state of mind. The state of primordial nakedness will only reveal itself in a state of non-conceptual awareness that is entirely free from contrivances and grasping, doubts and anticipation. Only in this state of naked awareness can we realize the meaning of primordially pure. To gain deeper understanding of the practice, we could to turn to the fifth chapter of the *Torch of the Eye of Meditation*, but it is outside the scope of our present discussion.

When meditating on threefold space, we can regard its primordial presence as infinite display and its clear light of purity as cognizance. This method of practice is adopted from my personal inner realization and was approved by my root guru, the venerable Dudjom Rinpoche. He explained that realizing the primordial presence of threefold space as infinite display indicates that this realization of primordial nakedness is beyond the four extremes. Such realization transcends the mind-itself and therefore surpasses the realization of naturally arisen phenomena as infinite display, which is attained from abiding in the mind-itself. Due to its transcendent nature, the attainment of the former realization is far beyond that of the latter. Dudjom Rinpoche stressed, however, that realizing the clear light of purity as the cognizant aspect would not transcend the fundamental clear light as defined by "spatial class" (Tib. *klong sde*) of the Dzogchen tradition. So how can we transcend it? Dudjom Rinpoche indicated that we should ground our realization according to the "pointing-out" instructions of the four liberations.

The Four Liberations

What are the four types of liberation? They are: one, primordial liberation; two, self liberation; three, instant liberation; and four, complete liberation. The teachings on the four liberations supplement threefold space meditation. After gaining some insight from threefold space meditation, we should try to sustain that experience during the post-meditation period and deepen it according to the general instruction of the four liberations. If we maintain our meditative focus both during and after meditation, we shall very soon realize the progressive stages of the path. The pointing instructions of the four liberations emphasize post-meditative practice following threefold space meditation. During that period, whatever thoughts arise, we can rest within them. Thoughts are naturally arisen expressions of the mind-itself. We let them arise, and they will dissolve back into its naturally liberating state. In our post-meditative practice, we sustain this naturally liberating state and allow our thoughts to arise and then dissolve. When a disturbing thought – for example, anger – arises, we recognize that it is a naturally arisen expression of the mind-itself. It arises because of the inherent capability of our primordial awareness. Since it is naturally arising, it can only be naturally liberated. It will not be stopped by the application of opposing force, nor will it vanish due to such effort. In this way, we spontaneously and nakedly realize the nature of anger. When we realize that it is unproduced, non-abiding, ungrounded, and neither coming nor going, we will spontaneously realize it is naturally-liberating and dissolves back into its own nature.

The mind spontaneously realizing its naturally-liberating state should be recognized as wisdom rather than as a state of mind. There are many classifications of wisdom states – four wisdoms, five wisdoms, two wisdoms and primordial wisdom are just some examples. However we classify them, they are but our naturally-liberating state of awareness. In this naturally-liberating state, the primordial clear light of purity will naturally manifest. It is the union of the aspect of cognizance and infinite displays, not separate from emptiness.

I would like to share with you a story about Garab Dorje (Tib. *dGa' rab rdo rje*), the first master of the Dzogchen lineage. Despite the antiquity of this event, it is full of insight for us today. Garab Dorje had a disciple named Majusrimitra. They met in Mount Wutai in China and stayed together for 75 years. When Garab Dorje was near parinirvana, Majusrimitra wailed and beseeched him to reveal the innermost essence of his teachings. Instantly, three rows of golden letters blazed across the sky:

> One is directly introduced to one's nature
>> (Tib. *ngo rang thog tu sprad*)
> One definitively decides upon this unique state.
>> (Tib. *thag gcig thog tu bcad*)
> One continues with direct confidence in liberation.
>> (Tib. *gdeng grol thog tu bca*)

Guru Padmasambhava later explained these statements as follows:

- When one can find nothing outside one's immediate awareness of the moment one is directly introduced to one's true nature.
- When one definitively concludes that immediate awareness of the moment is unproduced and naturally-liberating, one has decided directly upon this unique state.
- Having such affirmation, one continues with direct confidence in liberation.

These three rows of golden letters were later named "The Three Statements of Garab Dorje" or "The Three Statements that Strike the Essential Points" (Tib. *tsig gsum gnad du brdeg pa*). We can read numerous commentaries on the Three Statements. We must be careful, however, not to engage in too much in intellectual analysis because it may obscure the original meaning and intent. The true nature of all sentient beings is in the four liberating states. Our mental judgment, concepts and discriminations, however, prevent us from recognizing our original abode and realizing that we are primordially liberated. Because of that, the boundless becomes bounded, and openness is solidified. Because of that, we experience samsara.

These lines are excerpted from the *Tantra on the Penetration of Sound* (Tib. *sGra thal 'gyu*):

Your own awareness is free from conceptualization, so it is
endowed with the four great liberations.
As it is primordially liberated, it has no additional basis to
rely on.
(Original commentary: it signifies no modification.)
As it is naturally liberated, there are no antidotes.
(Original commentary: it signifies no investigation.)
As it is instantly liberated, it is liberated in its own state.
(Original commentary: it signifies resting in its own state.)
As it is completely liberated, there is no exertion.

Comparing the above with Padmasambhava's explanation of the Three Statements, we can clearly see that the Three Statements are the direct pointing-out instructions of the four liberations. They differ only in perspective. The essential meaning of the four liberations can be interpreted as the view, meditation practice, post-meditation practice and fruition of the path to enlightenment. Primordial liberation is the fundamental ground; natural-liberation is meditation without seeking or waiting, discrimination or judgment. Instant liberation is the instant dissolving of all naturally arising phenomena during our post-meditation practice. Complete liberation is realization attained without exertion.

The Three Statements reveal the path according to its nature, expressions and inherent capabilities. (We can also deem that as the view, meditation, and post-meditation practice, because the two groups of terms are interrelated.) The first statement, "One is directly introduced to one's nature," points out that from the nature of natural-arisen phenomena, one can determine that these phenomena are merely the immediate awareness of moments that instantaneously arise. The second statement, "One decides directly upon this unique state," indicates that the unique state of immediate awareness of the moments that one conclusively decides upon is the natural-liberation beyond the four extremes. The third statement, "One continues with direct confidence in liberation," reveals that all phenomena are naturally arisen and abide in the state of the four liberations. This is the inherent capability of all phenomena.

Besides explaining the commentary, I have a few words to add. When we engage in meditation, we have to base our practice on the mind-itself. There is no basis other than that. That is our constraint in this world of phenomena. We start, therefore, with the practice on the natural-liberation of *alaya* of the bardo of living. When we attain such liberation, we abide instantly in the mind-itself.

Then we progress to the practice on natural-liberation of delusion of the bardo of dreams. When our delusion is naturally liberated, we immediately recognize the delusive expression of the mind-itself. From this realization, the mind-itself is naturally liberated, and we abide simultaneously in the *dharmata*. Based on such attainment, the practice on the natural-liberation of the mind-itself in the bardo of meditation can effectively lead us to the natural liberation of *dharmata*, and allow us to abide simultaneously in the state of equanimity.

Advancing from natural liberation of the mind-itself to that of the *dharmata* involves transcending progressive stages of delusions. When we advance from abiding in the mind-itself to abiding in *dharmata*, our awareness expands to the infinite horizon. In the practice sense, we are transcending layer after layer of obstruction, from a state of naturally arisen mind-itself to naturally arisen *dharmata*.

The above summarizes the key teachings of the first three bardos. In review, we spontaneously realize the liberation of the mind-itself from the state of naturally arisen mind-itself; and we realize the liberation of *dharmata* from the state of naturally arisen *dharmata*. These progressive stages of practice are also mentioned in the Fourfold Cycle of Preparatory Practice in the *Dharma-dharmata-vibhaga* (*Distinguishing Phenomena and their True Nature*) composed by Bodhisattva Maitreya.

Doctrinal view must be combined with practice; otherwise it is mere intellectual speculation on names and concepts. On the other hand, if we practise without any theoretical understanding, it is difficult to relate our spiritual experiences to any meaningful perspectives. Either method of practice has its inherent shortcoming. Within its theoretical backdrop, I trust that scholars will not deem the four liberations as a doctrine refuted by Yogacara, or deem Maitreyan Yogacara as an independent teaching unrelated to Dzogchen's teachings.

We can now return to our discussion of the four liberations. Although the instructions on four liberations practice seem to have four different emphases, the four liberations actually occur simultaneously. For example, when a thought is primordially liberated, it is also simultaneously naturally liberated, instantly liberated and completely liberated. The same is true for the other liberations. We cannot separately apply instant liberation to liberate one state, and apply complete liberation to liberate another. The teaching is not intended to be applied that way. Similarly, although we have discussed liberation in terms of the mind-itself and of the *dharmata*, we cannot say, "I have now liberated the mind-itself," or "I have now liberated the *dharmata*." When we have attained the four liberations, the mind-itself (phenomena) and the *dharmata* (their true nature) will not be dualistically different from each other. In fact, when we realize the natural liberation of *dharmata*, the mind-itself must have already been naturally liberated. Realizing the four liberations means realizing the natural liberation of *dharmata*. When we actually attain such realization, there is no difference between the concept of liberation of the mind-itself and that of the *dharmata*. The main theme of the last of the Three Statements, "One continues with direct confidence in liberation," focuses mainly on our post-meditation practice. If we engage in post-meditation practice as described in the third statement, realization of the four liberations will arise spontaneously. Before that, though, our post-meditation practice has to be grounded on our formal meditation practice according to the second statement, "One decides directly upon this unique state," while in view of the first statement, "One is directly introduced to one's nature."

It is impossible to realize the four liberations by meditating solely on the threefold space. As soon as we consciously relate our meditation with having to experience "primordial," "clear light of purity," "emptiness" and "*rigpa*," we are automatically obstructed by such intellectual grasping. Although the grasping is subtle, it still precludes us from attaining liberation. To fill this gap, we supplement our post-meditation practice with the practice of the four liberations. During this, we observe the expression of our intrinsic luminous awareness (*rigpa*) in the aspect of emptiness, cognizance and infinite display not separated from each other. The *Tantra of the Studded Jewels* (Tib. *Nor bu phra bkod*) states, "When your pure consciousness manifests externally, its manifestations are naturally arisen appearances. At that moment, allow consciousness to express itself at ease." This means that when our pure consciousness is manifesting externally as naturally arisen expressions, we must allow it to express itself freely and easily before we can realize aspects of emptiness, cognizance and infinite display not separated from each other. (We can compare this with the state of undifferentiated decision in the bardo of living and alternate our practice between the two.)

The four liberations are not practice instructions; rather they are are attainments. Although we describe these attainments separately as realization of the view, meditation, post-meditation practice and resultant state, no concrete practice method can be taught. We would have completely misunderstood the Dzogchen teaching if we tried to apply a certain type of practice to a certain type of liberation. The post-meditation practice of the four liberations is like the action of Bodhisattva Avalokiteshvara, described in the *Heart Sutra*: "At that time, the noble one entered the meditative absorption on the appearance of the profound, seeing that even the five aggregates were empty of inherent existence." This is practice of the profound perfection of wisdom itself, and it is Yogacara. In other words, Bodhisattva Avalokiteshvara's "clearly beholding the practice of the profound perfection of wisdom itself" is the four liberations. The resultant state of the four liberations is the state Avalokiteshvara realized. We can take the *Heart Sutra* as a guide, showing us how to behold our practice after our formal meditation sessions. We continue on the path with confidence to realize spontaneously the essence of the perfection of wisdom – the perfect state of "no exalted awareness or wisdom, no attainment and no non-attainment."

The practice instructions of the threefold space and the four liberations in the teachings of the bardo of meditation are extremely profound. They are kept secret until the time comes for them to be revealed. We must practise them according to the directions of our root guru. Please bear in mind that it is impossible to attain realization by basing our practice on books alone. If we practise improperly, our psychological well-being may even be disturbed. I am emphasizing this again in closing this chapter to remind readers to be careful.

CHAPTER 14

The Bardo of Dying (Part 1)

Liberation through the Transfer of Consciousness

THE NEXT TEACHING IS ON THE FOURTH BARDO: the bardo of dying (Tib. *'chi'i kha bar do*). Its associated practices are divided into two levels. The easier practice is geared to the general practitioner while the more difficult one is geared to advanced-level practitioners. The goal of the easier practice is to transfer our consciousness to a Pure Land at the moment of our death; the goal of the advanced practice is to attain liberation through realizing the clear light of death (the clear light of *dharmata* or the clear light of primordial purity). There is a wide gulf between these two practices; we could even say they are light years apart. As with most of the teachings on the six bardos, only the less advanced practice is explained. It has been said:

> Some people do not have experience in its prior teachings such as illusory body, yoga of dream, clear light of purity, and so forth; while others have the requisite experience but do not understand the definitive meaning of the four clear lights. Especially for those such as the rich, the famous and the lazy, who have received profound teachings but lack the time to engage in formal meditation practice, Dharma is mere words on paper. For these people, natural liberation through transference of consciousness would be more appropriate. It would give them an opportunity to attain Buddhahood without the need of formal meditation practice.[1]

The easier general practice, which is simply a means to an end and not the essence of the teaching, is called "Natural liberation through transference of consciousness." What is meant by transference of consciousness? According to the Buddhist definition, it means the transfer of the consciousness of the deceased to one of the

---

1   *Cf.* Alan Wallace, trans., *Natural Liberation*, p. 195.

pure lands of the Buddhas. For example, when the consciousness of the deceased is transferred to the Pure Land of Amitabha Buddha, it takes rebirth there rather than in samsara. The Pure Land of Amitabha is not the only pure land. Buddha Shakyamuni said that there are countless pure lands. Among them, however, there are only two on which he placed importance. These are the Pure Land of Amitabha in the West, called *Sukhavati* or Pure Land of Ultimate Bliss, and the Pure Land of Akshobhya in the East, called *Abhirati* or Pure Land of Exceeding Great Delight. *Abhirati* is identical to the Pure Land of Vajrasattva, referred to by Vajrayana practitioners as *Akanishta*.

When our consciousness is transferred to a pure land, this does not mean that we have attained enlightenment. It means only that our consciousness is transferred to an environment more conducive to furthering our path. Think of it as comparable to transferring from a bad school, where a majority of the students have poor grades, to a good school, where most students can go on to prestigious universities. In a school with fine teachers and diligent students, we can make speedy progress.

Finding a favourable dwelling for the consciousness of the deceased is not an idea exclusive to Buddhism. In Hinduism, the *atman* – the soul or self of the deceased – may be released from suffering through uniting with the universal Brahman. In Judaism, through faith and good deeds, the soul will go to heaven upon death. The idea of salvation amongst these different religious doctrines is fundamentally similar, differing only on philosophical grounds. Strictly speaking, the transference of consciousness is merely a more advanced level of attainment, not liberation. After our consciousness is transferred, we still have to rely on ourselves to continue listening to, contemplating and practising Dharma in order to attain enlightenment; otherwise we will still be subject to cyclic samsaric rebirth. At this intermediate stage, we cannot rely on external help to attain liberation.

Among the practices of transference of consciousness, there is a more advanced practice that allows us to attain liberation at the moment of our death. This particular teaching is not about transferring our consciousness from one realm to another, from the samsaric world to a pure land; instead it is about instantly attaining the fruition of liberation. When we have not attained liberation through meditation during our lifetime, we can take advantage of the moment of our death to attain liberation. Because this practice can instantly liberate us from the bonds of samsara, it is considered extremely profound. Some do not believe that the attainment of liberation upon the moment of death or in the bardo state is possible. Yet, despite the impossibility of verification, the practice is endorsed by every spiritual tradition in Tibet; it has been accepted unquestionably for 1300 years. In addition, there are records from every tradition on such attainments from highly realized masters and sages. It would be rather difficult to promulgate a myth for this length of time without its falsehood being exposed.

The Tibetan Book of the Dead

As mentioned in chapter 6, from the entire series of texts on the six bardos, the companion volume, *Great Liberation in the Intermediate State through Hearing*, was translated into English under the title *The Tibetan Book of the Dead*, and published in 1927.[2] Over the course of more than 80 years of examination, the teachings contained therein have gained the respect of many scholars and researchers across the world (although as discussed below, scholars have some issues with the accuracy of the translation). Its teachings represent a quick and skilful way to attain liberation. When the teachings of the companion volume are combined with the rest of the instructions on the six bardos, one realizes the profundity of the entire collection.

How did the Tibetan esoteric teachings of *Great Liberation in the Intermediate State through Hearing* reach the Western world?[3] We need to go back to late 19th century New York, to the founding of the Theosophical Society by Madame Helena Petrovna Blavatsky (1832-1891), a Russian immigrant to the United States. Madame Blavatsky married at the age of 17. Just two months into her marriage, she left her husband to begin a lifelong quest for esoteric spiritual wisdom. At that time, due to rapid scientific and industrial development in the West, materialism had eclipsed traditional Western belief systems. As a result, spiritually hungry Westerners started travelling to the East in search of enlightenment. Blavatsky was one of these pioneers. She started her spiritual expedition in Cairo, travelled from Egypt to Sri Lanka, and then to India. She later went to Tibet and stayed for seven years.

In 1873, at the age of 41, Blavatsky claimed that she was instructed by a secret order of enlightened masters, the Mahatman, who lived in Tibet, to establish a Theosophical Society in New York. She first went to Paris and won financial support from a disaffected ex-Christian, and thereafter moved to the United States to expound the esoteric wisdom of Tibet. In response to Darwin's theory of natural evolution, Blavatsky developed a theory of spiritual evolution. She preached that

2   Evans-Wentz, The Tibetan Book of the Dead.

3   For a more detailed explanation, see Donald S. Lopez, Jr., *Prisoners of Shangri-La: Tibetan Buddhism and the West* (Chicago: The University of Chicago Press), pp. 46-85.

unity is fundamental in nature, and that in order to understand the law of nature and to expand the innate power of mankind, the spiritual evolution of mankind must synchronize with the growth of the universe. Blavatsky openly claimed to have gained this esoteric spiritual wisdom from the Mahatman in Tibet. The Theosophical Society received tremendous support and became an influential international organization. Over the course of ten years, it established more than 500 branches, spreading to over 40 countries. It had over 45,000 members and produced publications in several different languages.

The society and Blavatsky's works had a profound influence on Walter Evans-Wentz. As a teenage boy, he had already taken a great interest in spiritual books. Blavatsky's *Secret Doctrine*, which he read in his youth, had an enduring influence on him. After the publication of *The Tibetan Book of the Dead*, because its under-lying wisdom was in complete accord with the society's theories, Evans-Wentz was quickly recognized as head of the society.

From the point of view of today's scholar, Evans-Wentz's book is fraught with errors. Not only are there errors in translating words, there are numerous mis-statements of facts. In truth, the content of the book can hardly be considered a translation. As Evans-Wentz had never learned Tibetan, the work was translated under theosophical influence in collaboration with different translators of limited scholarly resources. The book was written primarily through the lens of theoso-phy, to introduce Westerners to the esoteric spiritual culture of the East. Despite the inherent inaccuracies in the book, it amassed a huge worldwide readership. Its popularity was an important milestone in history. Even Carl Gustav Jung, the famous psychoanalyst of the time, found it compelling. He said in his psychologi-cal commentary on the text:

> For years, ever since it was first published, the *Bardo Thodol* has been my constant companion, and to it I owe not only many stimulating ideas and discoveries, but also many fundamental insights... Its philosophy contains the quintessence of Buddhist psychological criticism; and, as such, one can truly say that it is of an unexampled superiority.[4]

In 1912, shortly after Jung's book *Symbols of Transformation* was published, his relationship with Sigmund Freud foundered. He resigned as chairman of the International Psychoanalytical Association and ended his six years of intense

4   Carl G. Jung, "Psychological Commentary on 'The Tibetan Book of the Dead'" (in *Collected Works of C. G. Jung*, 2nd edition, vol. 11), Princeton University Press, 1969, pp. 510-511.

collaboration with Freud. From that time on, Jung developed an intense interest in Eastern philosophy, which became the basis of many of his works of psychoanalysis. He wrote a commentary on an important Chinese Daoist book *The Secret of the Golden Flower*. Later, in the 1930s, his focus shifted from Chinese Daoist philosophy to Tibetan Buddhism. He was invited by Evans-Wentz to write a commentary for *The Tibetan Book of the Dead*. The original commentary, written in German and later translated into English, was included in the third edition. Following his commentary on *The Tibetan Book of the Dead*, Jung penned a series of writings closely related to Tibetan Buddhism. With shrewd judgment, Jung determined that the introversive psyche of people in the East is in stark contrast to the extroversive one dominant in the West. In his commentary, he declared: "In the East, the inner man has always had such a firm hold on the outer man that the world had no chance of tearing him away from his inner roots; in the West, the outer man gained ascendancy to such extent that he was alienated from his innermost being." [5]

Jung's relationship with Freud broke down over their diverging views on the nature of libido and the role of sexuality in human neuroses. Freud's psychoanalysis theory, grounded in childhood sexual fantasies, has critical constraints. Drawing a parallel with the teachings of the six bardos, Freud's rationale covers topics only up to the first bardo, the bardo of living. Aiming to break through the inherent limitations of Freudian psychoanalysis, and with an understanding of Eastern spiritual philosophy, Jung extends the theory of psychoanalysis to a point before the time of birth. The essence of his theory highlights the psychological aspect of the law of karma and rebirth, and leaps beyond the innate limitations of Western psychoanalysis. In the present day, certain psychotherapists may use therapies such as past-life regression and rebirthing to cure certain sicknesses. However, these therapeutic applications explore only the shallows of Jung's theory.

The theory behind Jung's psychoanalysis is closely related to the topic of the bardo of *dharmata* or reality, which is discussed in the following chapters. In the bardo of *dharmata*, the karma of the deceased will be reflected as different illusions. Based on his theory of the collective unconscious or *id*, common to all mankind, Jung explains karma psychologically in terms of psychic inheritance. Deep in our psyche lies a reservoir of our experience as a species. We evolve from the individual unconscious into the collective unconscious, and finally experience the timeless, formless, egoless state of complete freedom.

Thought understanding the historical background to *Great Liberation in*

5   Carl G. Jung, *Psychology and Religion: West and East* (in *Collected Works of C. G. Jung*, 2nd edition, vol. 11), p. 785.

the Intermediate State through Hearing, we can see how it took on the flavour of Jungian psychoanalysis. Not only was a psychological interpretation not the intended meaning of the original treasured text, but Evans-Wentz did not accurately translate its intended message.

Later, Lama Angarika Govinda, a German-born Indian who was a tenant of Evans-Wentz, wrote a foreword to his *Tibetan Book of the Dead*. Govinda enjoyed substantial influence over the spiritual community, and created a fad of using LSD to induce the state of liberation described in the book. He encouraged Westerners to forego their self-restraint to make progress on the journey of spiritual development. At Harvard University in 1960, lecturer Dr. Timothy Leary and Dr. Richard Alpert, a professor of psychology later known as Baba Ram Dass, began a research program called the Harvard Psilocybin Project to study the effects of psilocybin and LSD. They discovered that the psychedelic experience after taking LSD resembled the state of liberation described in *The Tibetan Book of the Dead*. Both Leary and Alpert were fired from Harvard in 1963. Undaunted by their dismissal, they continued their research at a private mansion. In 1964, Leary published a book called *The Psychedelic Experience: A Manual Based on the Tibetan Book of the Dead*. In it, he advocated the use of psychedelic drugs such as LSD to open the mind to transcendental experiences.

Further Adaptations

The original esoteric text of *The Tibetan Book of the Dead* was transformed from being a a set of guidelines for developing of inner realization to being a set of instructions in an outer pursuit of spiritual materialism, and further, to being a guidebook on how to use LSD. Although it differed vastly from the intention of the original Tibetan version, the translation gained unprecedented popularity amongst the spiritual community in the West, from highly respected scholars to laypeople. Filling the spiritual vacuum in Western society at that time, a highly respected Tibetan lama, Chogyam Trungpa, adapted the original treasured book into a Tibetan psychology text. Trungpa was born in 1940 in the Kham region of Tibet, and was well versed in the fields of art, psychology and comparative religion. He immigrated to the West and attended Oxford University. In 1973, he published *Cutting Through Spiritual Materialism*[6] and gained widespread popularity in the West. Based on the methods of psychotherapy, Trungpa's teachings became a very effective Dharma therapy for transcending the external craving for

---

6   Chogyam Trungpa, *Cutting through Spiritual Materialism* (Boston: Shambhala, 1973).

spiritual fulfillment. Trungpa reworked the translation of the *Great Liberation in the Intermediate State through Hearing*, creating a book of modern dharma therapy. Under his guidance, many Tibetan expressions were replaced by technical terms used in psychology, rendering it very difficult to relate to the original context of the treasured text. Trungpa deviated from the original text's teachings on the last three bardos, which include practices that mimic the different stages experienced upon death and before rebirth. In the original teaching, the various stages of dying, upon successive dissolution of earth, water, fire and wind, were explained to equip the practitioner for his dying day. However, Trungpa re-interpreted the four dissolutions in psychological terms of changes in emotional states.

In stark contrast to Trungpa's modern psychotherapy approach, the translation by Robert Thurman, the Je Tsongkhapa Professor of Indo-Tibetan Buddhist Studies at Columbia University, closely matches the intent of the original treasured text. Thurman was the first American Tibetan Buddhist monk in history and is well versed in the Tibetan language. Upon his return to America, he disrobed and became an important figure on the academic scene. Professor Thurman hesitated when considering a new translation of the *Great Liberation in the Intermediate State through Hearing*. However, recognizing the need of people close to death to learn about the dying process, he decided to translate the treasured text to articulate its intended teachings better. As a Je Tsongkhapa Professor, Thurman is an accomplished scholar who is naturally conversant with the teachings of the Gelug (Tib. *dGe lugs*) or Yellow Hat tradition. The Nyingma text of *The Tibetan Book of the Dead* was thus translated through the lens of the Gelug tradition. Unlike Trungpa's psychotherapy approach, Thurman explains the stages of death thoroughly in great detail. His book is titled *The Tibetan Book of the Dead: Liberation through Understanding in the Between.*[7] The name of the book reflects the intention of the original treasured text very well. To communicate with Western readers better, some Buddhist terms such as karma and Vajradharma are translated as evolution and Hero Scientist and so on. Interpreted from a non-Nyingma perspective, the Nyingma treasured text has become a modern Gelug writing. The entire collection of Nyingma supporting texts on the "Ordinary Preparation for Death" were largely neglected. The translation is primarily based on Je Tsongkhapa's *Lam tso rnam gsum*. The section on the Uncommon Preliminary Practices is also written not according to the Nyingma's practice tradition but to that of the Gelug tradition, rendering the book modern and Gelug.

---

7   Robert Thurman (trans.), The Tibetan Book of the Dead: The Great Book of Liberation Through Understanding in the Between, by Padmasambhava, foreword by the Dalai Lama (London: Harper Collins , 1994)

Seeing how the teachings of *Great Liberation in the Intermediate State through Hearing* have been disseminated in the West, we can conclude that the teachings on the six bardos have not been completely revealed. Because of the diverse background of the editors and translators, the translations of the topics on the Preparation for Death deviate to a large extent from the intended teachings of the Nyingma tradition. Nevertheless, the large audience attracted by the message of this treasured text has revealed how significant and profound its teachings are. Like the teachings of the Chinese *Yijing* or the Book of Change, its benefits are not only limited to Eastern philosophers but are available to readers from many walks of life. Whether militarists, politicians, historians or hallucinogenic drug experts, all can benefit from the teaching and expand their special areas of insight through the application of the *Yijing*.

Great Liberation in the Intermediate State through Hearing has undergone many transformations, from theosophy to psychotherapy to an important Gelug publication. It has also been referred to by many writers and thinkers in other fields. All have paid due respect to this treasured text as an important point of reference. The Buddhist explanation of the process of death and rebirth has become an accepted principle among many. Different parts of the treasured text have been adapted to the needs of different fields of study, reflecting the myriad applications of the theories on karma and reincarnation. In the following chapters, we shall introduce the treasured text from the Nyingma perspective.

CHAPTER 15

The Bardo of Dying (Part 2)

The Signs of Death

THE FIRST STEP IN THE BARDO OF DYING is to observe the signs of death. In an esoteric text called *Natural Liberation of Signs: Signs of Death*, part of the collection of teachings on the six bardos, the signs of death are grouped into six major types: external signs, internal signs, secret signs, distant signs, close signs and miscellaneous signs. There are lengthy explanations associated with each of these signs of death. To explain them in detail, it would be necessary to quote the above text in its entirety. Although I have translated it, I do not plan to have it published because many of the signs described in the text sound very superstitious by today's standards. For example, the text says that those who have signs of death will see their ancestors visiting them. While this sign of death may provide fertile material for Jungian psychoanalysis, to modern-day people, especially intellectuals, it simply sounds absurd and superstitious. I was once asked the following question about this: "According to Buddhist theory, the consciousness of the deceased will take the form of a bardo body and reincarnate in 49 days. If the bardo body has already been reincarnated after 49 days, then how could our ancestors, who all died a long time ago, appear before us?" To answer this, we need to first understand that the question mistakenly assumes that the appearance of an ancestor is an actual spirit. Secondly, it wrongly equates the spirit as a bardo body. The signs of death are merely illusions reflecting the subtle state of mind of the person who is about to die. That state of mind manifests itself as an illusion. This projected appearance is but an echo of the many psychological complexes lying deep within the mind.

Long ago, after the Chinese emperor Li Shimin (599-649 CE) of the Tang dynasty had taken the throne, he was constantly haunted by the spirits of those he had killed. Among them, the most hostile was his brother Li Yunji who often appeared with a copper sceptre, aiming to wreak vengeance on him. The prime minister, Weizheng, then asked two generals, Qin Shubao and Wei Cigong, to don full armour and stand by the palace gates to defend the emperor. After that, emperor Li was freed of the haunting spirits, and he never saw them again. Later, pictures of the two generals were engraved on the doors. They have been remembered ever since as the door gods, the spiritual guardians of the gate. From this ancient story, we can see how deeply we are affected by our own mind. When the right remedies are applied, the problems can be instantly dispelled. Not all signs of death are conclusive death signs; most of them can be remedied. An ancient text called *Natural Liberation of Fear: Cheating Death* provides extensive teaching on how to extend one's life. The practices include doing virtuous actions such as saving the lives of small animals that are about to be killed, and doing long-life practices such as Amitabha or purification practices such as Vajrasattva. Today, these practices would be considered psychotherapy; plumbing the deepest levels of the mind, they can hardly be considered superstitious.

Signs of Death According to the Vajrayana

In the following section, we shall selectively explain the six signs of death according to the Vajrayana tradition, focusing only on those which most people can relate to today.

1. External signs of death
   - Loss of appetite, symptoms of anorexia.
   - Deterioration of aural and visual faculties. When we focus our eyes, our ears cannot hear. When we concentrate on our hearing, our eyes cannot see.
   - Sudden, unpredictable rages wherein the emotions are unstable, the body moves violently and speech is abusive.
   - Becoming anxious and worried without good reason.
   - Being subject to nightmares.
   - Losing the shine of fingernails and toenails. In the most serious cases, the hair at the nape of the neck points up all the time, even after combing.
   - When sneezing mucus or ejaculating semen, feces and urine are uncontrollably excreted from the body at the same time.
   - The body begins to emit a pungent smell which cannot be washed away.
   - The bridge of the nose looks grey and lacks lustre.

- When fingers are pressed on the eyes, no sparks of light appear. If they do appear, they immediately fade away.
- When hands are pressed over the eardrums, no rumbling sound is heard.

The external signs of death are not conclusive indications of imminent demise. However, they are signs of serious problems that require immediate attention.

2. Internal signs of death
- When meditating in the Vairochana seven-point posture, you can only breathe through one nostril. For those who do not practise meditation, the same may happen during deep sleep. (This does not apply to those who practise completion stage breathing, which requires one to breathe in through one nostril and out through the other).
- Wind is slowly emitted from the mouth, nose and anus at the same time. This can be used to determine whether the sickness is serious or not.
- Deceased people seem to be constantly around, or deceased relatives frequently appear in dreams, living together in the same household.
- The following examples of ominous dreams are symbols of the internal signs of death – seeing oneself riding eastwards on a cat; seeing tigers or foxes riding southwards on a corpse; seeing oneself dressed in black and travelling downhill or down stairs; seeing oneself trapped in a cage or net; seeing one's body slit open by a woman and the heart taken out; seeing oneself sleeping soundly in a woman's womb; seeing oneself very old, yet tramping down the road bearing heavy loads; repeatedly seeing oneself falling into an abyss.

According to the teachings of Tibetan Buddhism, it is vitally important that, besides seeking medical help, people showing internal signs of death engage in the aforementioned Cheating Death Practice. It is also important to reinforce the will to survive in every way.

3. Secret signs of death
- For men, their semen turns black.
- Black spots appear on the penis.
- For women, their menses turn white.
- When she has menstrual problems, a woman repeatedly sees herself picking red flowers in her dreams.

People with secret signs of death may appear to be healthy, but at this point, the situation is already very serious. If a sick person sees the secret signs of death, it suggests that existing medical treatment is inappropriate. Under such circumstances, the Cheating Death Practice will not be of great help because the situation has deteriorated beyond the stage of being remedied by psychotherapeutic practices.

4. Distant signs of death
- On the 15th of the month, observe the shadow of your body under the moon when it is highest in the sky. If the shadow is flawless, then this is a good sign. Otherwise, you can determine your time of death from the position of the flaw.

5. Close signs of death
- Examples include the sudden failure of the five sense faculties, such as collapse of the bridge of the nose, loss of eyesight, black spots on the tongue, stiffening of both ears, and so forth.
- The body's waste products lose their warmth.

6. Miscellaneous signs of death
- When you gaze down, you cannot see the tip of your nose.
- When you look in the mirror, the eyes look blurry.
- When you blow air onto your palms, they feel cool instead of warm.
- When you take a shower, the chest is not wetted by water.
- When you snap your fingers, no sound is made.
- When you step on loose soil, no footprint can be found.

These are serious signs of death. At that point, it may be too late to apply the Cheating Death Practice to attempt a cure. People experiencing these signs of death should immediately practise transference of consciousness to insure against undesirable rebirth. You can tell if death is imminent by the following test. Place your fingers between your own eyebrows and gaze at your wrist. If the wrist appears to be dissected into two separate parts, this is a close sign of death; if it appears unusually slim, this is a distant sign of death. The thinner the wrist appears, the closer you are to your dying day. Under normal circumstances, the wrist should appear about one inch wide.

Through applying the above tests and carefully observing the signs of death, you can easily determine if the Cheating Death Practice can be used to cure underlying psychological problems that may be bringing about an untimely death. More importantly, from the observed result, a person can determine whether he should instead practise transference of consciousness to prepare for his death. Practising transference of consciousness without the occurrence of any sign of death is not recommended. It is equivalent to committing suicide and is as appalling as killing the Buddha. According to the rules, even when signs of death appear, one should first engage three times in Cheating Death Practice to see if the situation can be remedied. If the signs of death keep appearing, then you may engage in the practice of transference of consciousness.

In the process of dying, one undergoes the experience of dissolution of the four elements – earth, water, fire and wind – in successive stages. Upon completion of the final stage of dissolution, death is certain, and the clear light of death (primordial clear light) manifests. At that stage, you should either be prepared to welcome its manifestation or immediately engage in transference of consciousness. We will discuss these two practices in the following section.

The Four Dissolutions

This term four dissolutions refers to the dissolution of the four elements – earth, water, fire and wind – in our bodies. The earth element refers to the density and strength of our bones, cartilage, fingernails and so forth. The water element refers to our blood flow. The fire element refers to our body temperature, while the wind element refers to our breathing.

A dying person experiences the dissolution process in successive stages. In the first stage, the earth element dissolves into the water element. In this initial phase, the dying person feels like he is being crushed under a huge mountain. His body feels paralyzed. He perceives a mirage-like appearance resembling a shimmering river on desert sands. In the second stage, the water element dissolves into the fire element. The dying person feels cold and damp, as if he were immersed in icy water. Shortly, the icy conditions become hot and humid. He perceives a smoke-like appearance resembling smoke billowing out from a chimney. Then, the fire element dissolves into the wind element. The dying person feels as if he is being torn apart by a raging storm. He perceives a sparkling firefly-like appearance. Soon, his breathing ceases. When his gross wind stops, his nasal breathing ends, and he appears to be dead. However, this is not the end of the dying process because his consciousness has not yet left the body, and his inner wind is in the process of entering the central channel. The final stage occurs when the wind element dissolves into space element. At that stage, the inner wind dissolves into the central channel and the dying person experiences severe pain, as agonizing as a turtle being ripped alive from its shell. When the inner wind ceases, the consciousness leaves the body. This is when the dying process ends. Only at that moment can the person be considered genuinely dead. It takes about three and a half days from the time this gross wind ceases to the time his inner wind ceases. The duration depends on the individual's karma. The heavier the negative karma, the shorter the duration between the two stages.

How do we know when the inner wind has ceased? When the inner wind of a dying person starts to cease, a yellowish lymphatic fluid will begin to seep from one of his orifices. When this secretion has finished, the inner wind has completely ceased. It is clear that although the dying person has stopped breathing, his body should not be frozen before the yellowish secretion has completed its exit. Before his consciousness has completely left his body, uncomfortable environmental conditions can still produce a sensation of pain in the dying person's mind.

The Clear Light of Death

At which point does the clear light of death arise? To determine this, we have to look more closely at the stage of the dying process after the gross wind ceases. When the gross wind ceases, and the dying person stops breathing, he perceives a candle flame-like appearance. At the same time, the wind starts dissolving in his central channel. We call this the inner wind. When the inner wind first enters the central channel, his clear light mind starts glittering. At this point, if the dying person has practised the first three bardos under proper guidance during his lifetime, he can make use of the time the inner wind needs to dissolve in the central channel to evoke the primordial clear light of *dharmata*. This is the first appearance of the clear light of death.

The next stage is designated by the length of time the inner wind abides in the central channel of the dying person. It lasts about 30 minutes. This period shortens in relation to the dying person's negative karma. The heavier his negative karma, the less time the wind will abide in his central channel. During this period, the dying person experiences four successive stages of appearance called the Four Clear Lights of Emptiness. They are, respectively, the stages of appearance, increase, attainment and clear light. The last stage of clear light is the second manifestation of the clear light of death – the second time the dying person will perceive its appearance. The stages of appearance, increase, attainment and clear light manifest in sequence like moonlight at midnight, the break of day, twilight at dusk, and the light of dawn.

At the stage of attainment, the dying person's mind perceives the appearance of twilight at dusk, the hazy evening sky. He loses all sensory perceptions. There is no physical movement, no heartbeat. He looks as if he is already dead. Following this, the clear bright appearance manifests, resembling the light of dawn. We know this from the external sign: the yellowish secretion that passes out of one of the dying person's orifices. The internal sign is the inner wind reversing its direction, flowing from the central channel back to the left and right channels. When the inner wind reverses its flow, the stages of clear light manifest in reverse order: from attainment, to increase, then back to the stage of appearance. When it returns to the stage of appearance, the consciousness will depart from the body through the same opening the yellowish fluid used. At that time, the inner wind ceases and the dying process has ended. The consciousness enters the intermediate bardo state and takes on the form of a mental body. Slowly, it regains awareness, recalling the people and events of its lifetime. In a bardo state, the mental body can even see its body lying on the deathbed. This stage is no longer related to the clear light of death. However, this monotonous period of tedium can last a long time – up to three and a half days.

How to Abide in the Clear Light of Death

In the Nyingma tradition, abiding in the clear light of death is called *Dharmakaya* transference. We will discuss it briefly in the section covering transference of consciousness. First we will explain the commentary of *Great Liberation in the Intermediate State through Hearing* in a way modern people can understand.

The explanation deviates slightly from the tradition teachings of *Dharmakaya* transference.

As discussed in the previous section, the clear light of death first manifests when the dying person's gross wind stops and his inner wind starts dissolving in the central channel. If we wish to give guidance to the dying person, we should start the moment his gross breathing is about to cease. Repeat the instructions clearly, again and again. If possible, we should arrange the dying person to lie in the posture of the reclining Buddha:

- His head pointing north and his feet pointing south;
- Lying on his right side, with his right leg straight, and left leg slightly bent upon the right leg;
- His left hand resting on his left knee, or slightly bent covering the lower abdominal area below the navel;
- His chin resting on his right hand, his right little finger pressed against his right nostril and closing it.

These days, most people sleep on a soft pillow. In that case, the dying person can lie in the same posture by placing his right hand underneath the pillow. Rest his chin on the pillow, supported by his right hand. Close the right nostril by pressing the pillow against it. This is sometimes called the parinirvana posture – the posture Buddha Shakyamuni assumed when he passed to parinirvana.

We should give verbal instructions before the person stops breathing, so that he may stay focused and know the instructions by heart. It is very difficult to predict exactly when he will stop breathing, so we need to start before that moment occurs. We start by telling the dying person to follow the instructions with great faith. At the same time, we remind him to renounce worldly attachment and to generate *bodhichitta* (An altruistic wish to attain full enlightenment for the benefit of all sentient being).

Then, we guide him with the following verbal instructions:

"Please listen carefully. Very soon, the clear light of purity of the *dharmata* will manifest. You need to recognize this clear light.
"Death has arrived. The nature of the mind at death is pure. It is pure and thus empty. It is empty of solid existence, empty of form and colour.
"The emptiness of mind, and that of the *dharmadhatu*, are

called Samantabhadri of *dharmata* or primordial ground. It is so called because it is where all creations, all phenomena arise; like a mother who gives birth to sons and daughters.

"Now you need to observe your mind. During your lifetime, it has experienced many different obstructions which distorted and obscured its appearance. Because of this, you are unaware of its existence as primordial and luminous.

"From this mind of primordial clear light, also called Samantabhadri or primordial ground, arise countless phenomena. All these naturally arisen appearances are endowed with the aspect of cognizance and displays. You may not recognize this; you may mistake its natural cognizance to be a form of external appearance, and misinterpret its displays as the existence of external phenomena. In reality, the mind is pure, clear, and luminous.

"The aspect of cognizance and infinite displays are called Samantabhadra. It is the naturally arisen phenomena of the primordial ground.

"From this lucid clarity of mind, we can distinguish between different phenomena. Phenomena themselves have the inherent aspect of being differentiable. This differentiable characteristic is the aspect of cognizance in all naturally arisen phenomena. The crystal clarity of mind enables phenomena to naturally arise as infinite displays. However, when our mind is obstructed, we segregate our mind as the perceiver and all phenomena as external objects being perceived.

"The primordial ground, which is empty in nature, has never been separate from naturally arisen phenomena, which are endowed with the aspects of cognizance and display. Whether we are in this physical world or in the intermediate state, the two aspects have never been separated. We describe this as the union of Samantabhadra and Samantabhadri, personifying them in a form of sexual embrace.

"If you can recognize that the mind is Buddha, you should easily recognize that your mind has always been luminous, and abides in the clear light. Hence, you should be able to see yourself from your own mind. This is the secret meaning of abiding

the mind in Buddha. It means to abide in its three inseparable
aspects – emptiness, cognizance and displays; to abide in the
clear light of non-discriminatory awareness."

Guided by these instructions, the dying person can then recognize this self-realized, naked luminosity. The mind and clear light are neither separate nor one. When he attains certainty, he will be able to realize *Dharmakaya* liberation.

If the dying person cannot attain liberation upon the first manifestation of the clear light of death, then we need to offer another round of instructions upon its second manifestation. As explained previously, this lasts for about half an hour after the time gross breathing has stopped, while the inner wind abides in the central channel. This half-hour is a critical period. We need to remind the dying person repeatedly to recognize this clear light of death. Since it is difficult to determine exactly when the second clear light will manifest, we can administer a longer period of guided instructions for safety's sake.

We call the dying person by name, and repeat the instructions as before, again and again. Unlike the first clear light which manifests only at the instance the inner wind enters the central channel, we have about half an hour to prepare for the manifestation of the second clear light. This gives us more time to guide the dying person and remind him to visualize his personal deity. We tell the dying person:

"When you recognize your own mind, earnestly visualize your
personal deity. Remember that all phenomena are like reflections of the moon on water. Do not see them as solidly real,
otherwise your mind will be obstructed, and its luminosity
obscured."

After this, the next stage is the long, tedious period of three and a half days that we described earlier. During this time, the inner wind reverses its flow from the central channel out to the left and right channels. The clear light of death also reverses its sequence. During this period, we can give intermittent sessions of verbal instruction. Above all, we should instruct the dying person in the details of generating himself as his personal deity. If he can achieve this, it is very possible that he will attain liberation through attaining the pure illusory body.

We have not yet finished with the bardo of dying. We will continue our discussion of the transference of consciousness practice and its applications in the next chapter.

CHAPTER 16

The Bardo of Dying (Part 3)

The Practice and Actual Undertaking of Transference of Consciousness

THE CORE TEACHING OF THE BARDO OF DYING focuses on the practice and the actual undertaking of transference of consciousness. This topic often stirs up a storm of questions on faith and belief. When talking about transference of consciousness, many Buddhists immediately associate *Sukhavati* or the Pure Land in the West as the destination. Followers of other religions reject the idea of a pure land entirely, and have their own versions of heaven. Agnostics may view belief in Buddha and the Pure Land as similar to belief in God, and even denounce the concept as some kind of superstition. To clear the air, let me first clarify what is meant by transference of consciousness.

Transference of consciousness to the Pure Land is not the only method of transference of consciousness within the Buddhist tradition. Neither is it one that will lead to liberation. Unlike the transference of consciousness taught by the six bardos, which is a method of attaining liberation, transference of consciousness to the Pure Land as followed by the exoteric tradition leads only to another state of existence. According to the exoteric tradition, the consciousness of the deceased is reborn immediately in the Pure Land without going through the bardo state in the form of a mental body. Although consciousness has taken rebirth in the Pure Land of the Buddha, it cannot immediately or naturally manifest itself. It has to remain in an embryonic state, like a lotus bud waiting for the chance to blossom into a flower to meet the Buddha. When the conditions are right, it naturally manifests itself in the Pure Land. However, this naturally arisen appearance is still not the attainment of nirvana. It has yet to listen to Dharma, contemplate its meanings, and practise accordingly in order to attain liberation.

When we understand fully, we can see that Pure Land is not a spurious concept. Countless realms exist, but do not arise from the karma of sentient beings. Buddhists do not deny either the existence of Hindu deities such as Brahma, Shiva, Indra and others or their pure lands. They can be established as existing because, whenever someone believes in the deities, the karma which allows their realms to arise will be established. Following this reasoning, when Buddha said there is such a thing as Pure Land, it was able to come into existence. Similarly, when God said "Let there be light!" there was light. Both Pure Land and light are established from karma. According to the Buddhist view, however, realms established by the karma of sentient beings arise with constraints. Sentient beings in pure lands are not free from these constraints. If the sentient beings there cannot attain enlightenment, then they are still subject to the constraints of cyclic existence. In the same way, if we do not attain enlightenment, our karma causes us to take rebirth in samsara again and again. In Buddhism, sentient beings in pure lands have to practise further to attain enlightenment; this distinguishes Buddhism from other religions that consider heaven, which is a kind of pure land, to be the final destination.

The teachings on transference of consciousness in the six bardos transcend the concept of Pure Land. Within its five practices, three can actually lead to liberation. These are *Dharmakaya* transference (transference of Truth body), *Sambhogakaya* transference (transference of Enjoyment body), and *Nirmanakaya* transference (transference of Emanation body).

How can we apply the practice of transference of consciousness to attain liberation upon the moment of death? At death, there is a short space of time in which our consciousness is free from the constraints of our five aggregates. This moment is a great opportunity to free ourselves from the obstructions of our deluded thoughts. If we miss this chance, then our mental continuum forms a mental body in the bardo state, and obstacles to liberation arise once again. Liberation can be attained in that short moment by relying on the practice of transference of consciousness during our lifetime. This kind of practice is very different from those based upon religious beliefs. The practice of transference of consciousness is also known as *phowa* (Tib. 'pho ba). Although this practice is commonly taught, most teachings focus only on the exit of the consciousness of the deceased through the Brahma aperture, to be reborn in a Pure Land. Teachings on the actual undertaking of attaining liberation through transference of consciousness are, in fact, quite rare. The methods explained in the six bardos are those very rare teachings.

The nine apertures

Buddhists believe that upon our death, there are specific exits through which our consciousness leaves the body. These are usually called the nine apertures, or nine doors; however, sometimes, because a pair of eyes can count either as a single aperture or as two apertures, ten apertures are spoken of. In this text, we speak of nine.

The upper three apertures

There are three upper apertures, the Braham aperture at the crown, the eyes taken together as one aperture, and the left nostril. When the consciousness of the deceased leaves through the Brahma aperture, it attains Dakini Pure Land, the state of natural liberation of *rigpa*. Success depends on correct practice during our lifetime. Even if we can cause the Brahma aperture to open enough to allow for the insertion of a blade of kusha grass, unless we have practised correctly, the consciousness may leave through one of the other apertures. When the consciousness of the deceased leaves through the eyes, it is reborn as a world monarch, a being of great power. At this time, the mind is in a defiled state. The same holds true for the third upper aperture, being the left nostril. When the consciousness of the deceased leaves through the left nostril, it is reborn as human. Assuming the Sleeping Buddha posture with the right hand supporting the head and the right little finger covering the right nostril is conducive for rebirth as human. The right nostril is a different matter entirely.

The middle three apertures

The three middle apertures are the right nostril, the ears and the navel. When the consciousness of the deceased leaves through the right nostril, it is reborn as a Yaksa (nature spirit). When it leaves through the ears, it is reborn as a god or goddess in Realm of Form. When it leaves through the navel, it is reborn as a god or goddess in the Realm of Desire.

The lower three apertures

The three lower apertures are the openings of sex and elimination. When the consciousness of the deceased leaves through the urethra, it is reborn as an animal. When it leaves through the genital aperture, it is reborn as a hungry ghost (the genital aperture refers to the penile opening for men or the vaginal opening for women), and when it leaves through the anal aperture, it is reborn as a hell being.

Meditation of Body

The initial step in the practice of transference of consciousness is to leave the Brahma aperture unblocked while blocking the other eight apertures. To begin this practice, we sit comfortably on a cushion. It is not necessary to sit in a seven-point Vairochana posture. The elderly may recline in bed, preferably in the Sleeping Buddha posture. If we are sitting, we should place hands on knees, straighten our backs and level our shoulders. We should visualize a luminous dark blue syllable HUM at the heart chakra. This syllable HUM emits another syllable HUM, which descends to our anal aperture, blocking the door to the hell realm. Then the syllable HUM at our heart then emits a second syllable HUM, which descends to the genital aperture, blocking the door to the realm of hungry ghosts. The syllable HUM at the heart chakra emits a third HUM, which descends to the urethra aperture to block the door to the animal realm. It is very important to block the doors to the lower three realms. We should practise this repeatedly, until we are so familiar with it that we can effortlessly emit the syllable HUM three times to block off the three apertures.

We must repeat this practice to block off the other five apertures that are the exits to samsaric rebirth: the navel, the two nostrils, the two ears and the pair of eyes. In this practice, we also need to block off the mouth aperture although it is not a door through which the consciousness departs. The mouth aperture is, however, the top blocking point of the defiled wind and the life wind. Lastly, we should visualize a white inverted syllable HAM at the Brahma aperture (a measurement of eight fingers from the hairline), blocking it too. This is the meditation of body. Nyingma tradition places heavy emphasis on this practice because it is the foundation to the practice of forceful transference of consciousness.

The forceful transference of consciousness practice is used to cope with untimely death. When death is imminent – for example, when the heart stops beating – the dying person has little time to prepare for the moment. He is already experiencing the sequential signs of death. Under such circumstances, he can only practise the forceful transference of consciousness to attain liberation. Even if liberation cannot be attained through the practice, the practitioner will at least be protected from falling into the three lower realms.

If the dying person is familiar with the practice of blocking the apertures, then there is no need for him to visualize them one by one. Instead, he should visualize the root guru sitting on the Brahma aperture. This visualization arouses a mind of faith, which eases the fear of death. The dying person then radiates light from his heart chakra, which fills his body, automatically blocking the apertures except for the Brahma aperture. By this means, the mind of the dying person is naturally placed at the crown. The key to the forceful transference of consciousness is to remember one's guru wholeheartedly.

Of course, we still need to practise during our lifetime. To practice, we can envisage some near-death situations. For example, we might imagine that we are falling from a cliff. In a state of great fear, we should instantly remember to recall our guru sitting on our Brahma aperture, and then examine our drops to see if they are rushing to our crown of their own accord. We can even make use of any sudden, unexpected occurrence in our daily life. For example, if a sudden loud noise startles us, we can use the moment immediately to recall our guru sitting on our crown. It is very beneficial to practise the forceful transference of consciousness. If we are familiar with the practice, it will not only help us not in a sudden-death situation, but also in our normal death. We can also help those who are dying by giving them guidance in the forceful transference of consciousness.

Meditation of Wind

Meditation of wind is widely accepted as part of the practice of transference of consciousness, but the teachings vary among different traditions. Here we will discuss only the practice according to the teachings of the six bardos.

First, we sit in the seven-point Vairochana posture. Then we visualize our central channel, running from just below the secret place (the width of four fingers down from the navel) to the Brahma aperture at our crown. The central channel is straight and saturated with wind, like a long, thin, puffy lamb intestine. It is suffused with light, white in colour with a touch of yellow, luminous and bright. The visualization practice is not very difficult. Some elderly people with no prior training in meditation can clearly visualize the channel after practising two or three times. The key is to straighten the back. When the back is straightened, we can easily visualize the central channel to be straight and luminous. We next visualize our root guru, in the aspect of our personal deity, sitting on our crown. At the same time, we visualize a luminous drop at our navel chakra. We recite HIG KA seven times while drawing the drop up from the navel chakra to the heart chakra. We recite HIG KA another seven times while drawing the drop up from the heart chakra to the throat chakra. We repeat the HIG KA seven times more while drawing the drop up from the throat chakra to the chakra between the eyebrows. We should make these 21 recitations in one breath. Then, taking a breath, we repeat HIG KA seven times more, making the very last one very loud. As we do this, the drop ascends to the HAM at the Brahma aperture and stays there. After remaining keeping the drop at our Brahma aperture for a while, we conclude the practice by letting it descend to the navel chakra.

This is the traditional practice of *phowa*. Details vary, however, among different traditions. The details are usually transmitted verbally by the lineage master. Verbal instructions are very important. It is said that this practice may shorten our lifespan if practised without direct verbal instruction from a qualified master. Because there is such a danger, it is not included as the main practice among the most esoteric teachings in the Nyingma tradition. Instead, another method is used that does not risk shortening the lifespan. This profound method is described in many Tibetan Buddhist hagiographies, which record that when the dying master cried out AH in one long breath, auspicious signs such as a rainbow immediately appeared in the sky. This is the actual undertaking of the esoteric transference of consciousness, as opposed to mere practice. With this practice, there is no need to open the Brahma aperture; neither is there a danger of shortening our lifespan.

Meditation of Mind

The meditation of mind in the transference of consciousness is relatively simple. As with the meditation of wind described previously, we place our mind on the movement of the white drop in the central channel. The key instruction is this: when the drop ascends, it moves in a straight, direct manner; but when it descends, it circles down slowly, forming a spiral of white light. This spiral of light slowly dissolves (but does not dissipate) into the central channel, like water mixing with water. It is best if, at the same time, we visualize our guru sitting on our crown.

Some people wonder why having a guru is so important in Tibetan Buddhism. Usually, followers of a religion regard holy beings as more important than living teachers. Even followers of exoteric traditions such as Pure Land are only required to visualize the holy beings of the Western Pure Land when reciting the sutras or the name of the Buddha, and not the guru. Why then is Tibetan Buddhism so different? The question touches on a very deep topic. In any practice, Buddhas and personal deities are symbolic representations. Each personal deity has a symbolic meaning, which is related to various positive states of mind. In this same cycle of treasure texts discovered by Karma Lingpa, the generation-stage practice related to the teachings of six bardos[1] establishes 100 peaceful and wrathful deities directed towards our grasping of elements (e.g. grasping the elements of earth, water, fire, wind and space), our grasping of psychological states (e.g. grasping of self), and our grasping of various mental states, which, according to the Yogacara school, are called mind and mental factors. Even for the Pure Land tradition, we need to look at the meanings behind the symbols. For example, when, through the force of aspiration, a practitioner transfers his consciousness to *Sukhavati*, the Pure Land in the West, then in that realm, the karma of aspiration will predominate.

On the other hand, aspiration is not sufficient for taking rebirth in *Abhirati*, the Pure Land in the East. The practitioner must have also attained an immovable (*vajra*) state of mind. *Vajra* means unswerving, unchanging. A *vajra* state of mind is a mind that stays pure amidst a world of greed, hatred and delusion. It remains unaffected in the face of all deluded karma. Akshobya and Vajrasattva, who symbolize this flawless, unchanging, immovable, indestructible nature, are the Buddhas associated with *Abhirati*, the Pure Land in the East.

When we practise, it is important to contemplate the meaning associated with these symbols, in order that our mind be transformed. If we grasp onto the mere appearance of a deity, we will at best feel a little more positive. No matter how much our feelings are improved, our underlying psychological makeup will not have changed in any sense.

But still, how does that make the root guru so important? The root guru is merely a symbol, but a very important one. The guru acts as a bridge that enables the practitioner to cross from an ordinary state of mind to the wisdom state symbolized by enlightened beings. When we say "Guru stands for Buddha," it is like saying "The Golden Gate Bridge stands for San Francisco." In this context, the guru is like a landmark. Because of this, we must first visualize our root guru and then visualize our root guru in the aspect of our personal deity. This rule applies to all *Anuttarayogatantra*, but is not applicable to the practices of the lower three Tantra systems because, in them, personal deities are not established as symbolic states of mind.

In the practice of transference of consciousness, therefore, it is essential to have a clear appearance of the guru sitting on our crown, from which we visualize him in the aspect of our personal deity (for example, Vajrasattva). Non-Buddhist practitioners can visualize the holy being of their own religion upon their crown. Upon death, a practitioner must let the luminous drop in the central channel shoot up to the heart chakra of the personal deity or holy being.

---

1   Included in the texts are *Natural Liberation of the Psycho-physical Aggregates* (Phung po rang grol gyi don bsdus) and *Natural Liberation of Habitual Tendencies* (Tib. *Bag changes rang grol*).

Dharmakaya Transference

In the following sections, we will discuss the actual undertaking of transference of consciousness. The first we will attend to is the *Dharmakaya* transference. Before we begin the main practice, it is best to first establish our motivation. For Buddhist practitioners, it is essential to generate *bodhichitta*. With a heart of compassion, we are engaging in the practice of transference of consciousness to attain liberation for the benefit of all sentient beings.

In helping a dying person transfer his consciousness, we must remember to make sure that there are no sentimental or material belongings to which the dying person may be emotionally or psychologically attached, next to him.

I remember an old story my father told me. He had a friend who had engaged in Pure Land practice for over 30 years. When the friend was dying, many of his friends gathered around to recite Namo Amitabha with him. In the beginning, he looked calm and peaceful, lying in the Sleeping Buddha posture with a smiling face. Suddenly, his smile was gone, and he started to furrow his brows, frowning and struggling to open his eyes. His friends were astonished, and wondered what caused him to behave like this. Later they discovered that it was because of two jade pendants he had touched when he had put his left hand on his left thigh. The two pendants were his favourite antiques, and had been hanging from his waist for a long time. His family members thought they should not take them away from him, so they had left them on him. It is commonly believed that keeping the favourite items of the dying person close to him will bring him peace. However, the opposite is true. Doing so only arouses a mind of desirous attachment and distracts the person from making good use of the moment of death to attain liberation through the actual transference of consciousness. My father asked the family members to take the two jade pendants off his friend's waist and to take away all the other items he treasured. Once they were gone, the dying man could concentrate on the visualization of clear light. Those who are familiar with the meditation on clear light during their lifetime can achieve the visualization through their own efforts.

This visualization practice is technically called the "union of mother clear light and child clear light." Mother clear light is the manifestation of the clear light of *dharmata*. It appears primordially since beginning-less time. However, under the veil of our delusions, we cannot recognize its appearance. As discussed before, three and a half days after a person has passed away, this clear light will manifest twice (first when the gross wind ceases, and then when the inner wind ceases). If, during these two critical times, the deceased can manifest the child clear light in his heart, it will instantly connect to the mother clear light, like a drawbridge that has suddenly been lowered, allowing a child to run back to his long-lost mother. Upon this union, one can attain *Dharmakaya* liberation through transference of consciousness. Child clear light is the intrinsic luminosity of our mind, attained from meditation practice. It is not primordially existent, and because of that it is sometimes referred to as clear light of the path. If we practise diligently in our lifetime, and if we are able to maintain a pure state of mind unsullied by the five poisons (greed, anger, delusion, jealousy and pride), then upon our death, the child clear light will naturally manifest, waiting for the mother clear light (the clear light of death which manifests twice) to arise, in order to attain the natural union.

The purpose of our regular practice of visualizing the luminous drop at our heart chakra is to familiarize ourselves with its manifestation, so that upon our death the child clear light will promptly arise. If the clear light of the path (i.e. child clear light) manifests effortlessly in our meditations on the bardo of living, the bardo of dreams and the bardo of meditation, then the primordial clear light of *dharmata* (mother clear light) may also arise. Under such circumstances, we can realize the union of mother and child clear light before our death.

Sambhogakaya Transference

If the practitioner has experience of generation stage practice – or has received teachings on the completion stage practice of transference of consciousness – but has not recognized emptiness, then it will be more beneficial to practise *Sambhogakaya* transference.

What do we mean by recognizing emptiness? As we have discussed previously, emptiness has to be realized through its cognizance and infinite displays, just as in daily life we realize the nature of water through its appearance and function. Similarly, emptiness cannot be realized in the absence of its expression (cognizance) and inherent capabilities (infinite displays).

There are two kinds of practitioners who experience major difficulties in realizing emptiness. The first kind grasps onto the apprehended (the expression) and what apprehends. They are misled by dualistic constraints of object and subject. The second kind recognizes the cognizance and infinite displays of phenomena, but cannot realize that the three aspects – emptiness, cognizance and infinite displays – are in unison. According to the *Heart Sutra*, the former has not realized "form is emptiness, emptiness is form"; the latter has not realized "emptiness is not other than form, form too is not other than emptiness." Both have failed to realize the essence of the profound Prajnaparamita. For the former practitioner, it is difficult to be certain that the clear light of path (child clear light) will arise upon his death; for the latter, although the clear light of path (child clear light) will arise, it is difficult to be sure that it will be able to connect with the manifestation of the primordial clear light of *dharmata* (mother clear light) in order to attain a union. This is the case because once the practitioner conceptualizes the three aspects – nature of emptiness, its cognizance and its infinite displays – the clear light of path becomes unstable.

To solve this problem, we have to gain familiarity with, and rely on, our practice during our lifetime. First, we block the apertures with the seed syllables; then we utter HIG KA to make our mind (the luminous drop) ascend to the syllable HAM at our Brahma aperture. At this time, the syllable HAM is not inverted. The Brahma aperture will naturally open. At the same time, we visualize our root guru, who is sitting on our crown, in the aspect of our personal deity. We utter HIG KA, and then shoot our mind, the pure white drop, up from our heart chakra to that of our root guru. We rest our mind, the luminous white drop, in our root guru's heart. If our gross wind ceases while we are abiding in this state, we attain the fruit of *Sambhogakaya* Vajradhara, which is non-dual with our personal deity.

Nirmanakaya Transference

Buddhists who have not practised Vajrayana meditation in their lifetime can only practise *Nirmanakaya* transference. First, we lie in the Sleeping Buddha posture, with our head pointing north. We try to breathe only through the left nostril. If possible, we place a picture of our guru or a *thangka* of the personal deity within the vicinity. If this is not convenient, we should try visualizing one or other of them. Normally, we should be able to at least clearly visualize our guru. At this time, people around the dying person should pray, "Relying upon this practice, may I attain the *Nirmanakaya* for the sake of all sentient beings, and bring the benefits to the whole world." If possible, the dying person should try to visualize the navel chakra in the form of a tetrahedron-shaped womb and, at the same time, also maintain a clear appearance of the central channel. Inside it, there is a luminous white drop with a tint of red radiating from inside. We recognize this glittering drop as being in the nature of the primordial wisdom. We raise our pelvic floor muscles, and drive the wind upward. We should try our best to recite

HIG KA repeatedly, and, at the same time, raise the white drop to the left nostril. Then, instantly, we merge our mind together with our wind into the heart chakra of the *Nirmanakaya* of the personal deity, and allow our mind and wind to settle there in peace. We should repeat this many times, until we can do it no more. When the wind ceases, the deceased will not enter the bardo state. His inner wind will abide in the central channel and will not revert back to the left or right channel. This way, he will definitely be reborn as a human who will be able to benefit other sentient beings. His rebirth will be determined by his attainments.

Mundane Transference

Those who have faith in Buddhism but have not engaged in any practices at all can only practise the mundane transference of consciousness. The dying person should rest with his head pointing north. Just this mere positioning will bring him great benefits. If possible, he should receive an empowerment from his guru. Family members may lightly caress the Brahma aperture of the dying person. At times, they may even lightly pull the hair at the Brahma aperture and tell him gently "Buddha is sitting here, waiting for you." In addition, they can recite Namo Buddha Ratnasikhin, Namo Bhaisajyaguru. (Pure Land followers can recite Namo Amitabha.) Vajrayana practitioners can recite the One-Hundred-Syllable Mantra, the Six-Syllable Mantra and the Heart Mantra of Vajrasattva. Followers of other religions can recite the name of their holy being, or act according to the traditions of their religion. Practising this way, the deceased is protected from falling to the lower three realms, and may be reborn in the human or god realms.

CHAPTER 17

The Bardo of *Dharmata* (Part 1)

Fear and Away From Fear

AFTER EXPERIENCING THE BARDO OF DYING for three and a half days, the consciousness of the deceased, the bardo being, takes on the form of a mental body and undergoes a further 15 days of the bardo of *dharmata*. This period is divided into two stages. The first stage lasts only about half a day, ending four days after the gross wind ceases. During this time, hallucinations, which arise from the bardo being's karma, appear vividly to the mind. The second stage consists of two seven-day cycles. It starts roughly on the fifth day after the gross wind ceases and ends on the 18th day. During this stage, the mental body experiences illusions of both peaceful and wrathful deities.

In earlier chapters we looked in detail at the aspects of emptiness, cognizance, and infinite displays of phenomena. Of these three aspects, we can directly realize only the cognizance and infinite displays. Emptiness must be realized indirectly, through practices involving the other two aspects. As with the example of water, we can only realize its nature by observing its various appearances and functions. This is the purpose of the practice of the bardo of *dharmata*, the ultimate nature of all phenomena; the attainment of the practice is called the natural liberation of infinite displays. We begin by realizing emptiness through the aspects of cognizance and infinite displays. We then recognize that the three aspects are in fact inseparable, not different from each other. Although we call the attainment from this practice the natural liberation of infinite displays, it is accomplished by simultaneously observing the aspects of both infinite displays and cognizance.

The analogy of an abandoned baby who is sleeping and has not yet woken up has been used to describe the state of *dharmata*. It implies a state that is removed from suffering and fear. Even though the baby has been abandoned, if he remains in a deep sleep, he will not feel any suffering. If the poor baby wakes, however, he will suffer as a result of coming into contact with various samsaric phenomena. Reflecting on this, we can see that the suffering we experience in this world and the fear the mental body faces in the bardo state are like the feelings the baby experiences when he wakes. Although we are just like that abandoned baby, if we can realize that emptiness, cognizance and infinite displays are not separate from each other, we can be without suffering and free from all fear.

I will now discuss the various phenomena that occur in the two stages of the bardo of *dharmata*, and then proceed to discuss its practice. When the deceased misses the two opportunities to realize the clear light of death, he arises in the form of a mental body in the bardo of *dharmata*. The bardo of *dharmata* has two stages. Fearsome hallucinations occur in both. In the first stage, brilliant lights, blinding flashes and thundering sounds occur simultaneously. The light is as bright as a thousand lamps blazing into the eyes; the flashes are as dazzling as a thousand forks of lightning; the noise is as deafening as a thousand claps of thunder. During his lifetime, the deceased never experienced such a terrifying situation; his mental body is overwhelmed by terror. In panic, it tries to escape; it runs until it is totally exhausted and then passes out.

The second stage has two seven-day cycles. In the first cycle, peaceful deities appear to the mental body. However, the lights, flashes and noise from the first stage continue, and the mental body cannot remain with the peaceful deities. The deities are white, blue, yellow, red or green depending on their Buddha family, hold symbolic implements, make different hand gestures or *mudras*, and wear garments that have deep symbolic meaning. In the second cycle, the lights, flashes, and noise intensify, and terrifying wrathful deities, in different colours, possibly with several heads, or multiple arms and legs, appear. When the mental body sees peaceful or wrathful deities, it should instantaneously realize that they are naturally arisen displays, beyond the dimensions of time and space, full of aliveness and symbolic meaning. However, the mental body may be panic-stricken, and strongly tempted to escape to a less intense environment. As a result, it throws itself back into the samsaric realm by taking rebirth.

These descriptions of the experiences of the mental body in the bardo of *dharmata* may seem mystical and superstitious to modern people. Acknowledging this, I will briefly explain the meaning behind the concept to dispel certain common misconceptions. There is a famous story about the Chan master Huineng, who was the sixth patriarch. After receiving special teachings from the fifth patriarch, Hongren, Huineng secretly travelled to the south of China. He went to Guangzhou and stayed for many years at the Guangxiao Monastery without disclosing his true identity. At the monastery one day, the Chan master Yinzong was expounding teachings on the *Mahaparinirvana Sutra*. When he was halfway through his lecture, he suddenly pointed to a large Dharma flag fluttering in the breeze, and asked the class to describe the situation. One disciple said, "The flag flutters." Another said, "The flag is inanimate. It flutters because of the wind." This answer was poorly reasoned, and as soon as it was given, someone rebutted it, saying, "The wind cannot move. It is also inanimate. The flag flutters because of the ripening of karmic causes and conditions of both the wind and the flag." Suddenly, Huineng called out, "It is your mind that flutters." The entire class was amazed and impressed by his wise reply. Huineng then revealed his real identity as the sixth patriarch of the Chan tradition. From that day on, Master Yinzong and his disciples followed Huineng as their teacher, and began what became known as Chan Buddhism. (Before Huineng, the tradition had been known as the Lanka School.)

Hearing this story, many people today misunderstand Chan Buddhism as being a proponent of the Cittamatra "mind only" view that says that no phenomenon exists external to or independent of the perceptions of our mind. Others erroneously consider Chan Buddhism to be a proponent of the "subjective mind only" view that says all phenomena are projections of our subjective mind. This is a complete misunderstanding of Chan Buddhist philosophy.

Let us examine the story. Those who said "The flag flutters" are very objective. When they saw the flag move, they believed it moved of its own accord. This is what ordinary people would commonly think. Those who said "The flag is inanimate – it flutters because of the wind" hold the view of the Cittamatrins. However, the way the answer is framed has a major flaw. The first phrase, "The flag is inanimate," fits the view of the Cittamatrins that all external phenomena are perceived in accordance with the karmic propensity of our mind. However, the second phrase, "It flutters because of the wind," directly contradicts the first. But if we say that the flag is inanimate, then the wind must also be inanimate because both flag and wind are external phenomena. For this reason, we cannot conclude that "It flutters because of the wind." Those who have misunderstood the views of the Cittamatra and Maitreya-Yogacara schools often draw this conclusion. Those who said "The flag flutters because of the ripening of their karmic causes and conditions" take the view of Madhyamaka School that all phenomena arise from the ripening of karmic causes and conditions; because there is a flag plus wind, the phenomenon of the fluttering flag arises. This view reflects the teachings of Nagarjuna, whose teachings are regarded as examples of advanced Buddhist philosophy, able to withstand rigorous logical analysis, even by present-day scholars. The concept of karma – of causes, conditions and effects – is, in fact, very scientific. A seed (the cause) cannot sprout by itself. It must also have the necessary conditions present, such as having been planted in the soil and having the right amount of sunlight, water, before it can ripen and bear fruit. Nagarjuna's teachings that "things do not arise from one single cause" and that "one single cause not complemented by any other conditions cannot give rise to any phenomenon" are irrefutable.

However, when Huineng said, "It is your mind that flutters," he is not holding either the "mind only" view or the "subjective mind only" view. His statement is drawn from observation of the arising of phenomena. There is no need to debate whether or not phenomena that arise from karmic causes and conditions exist because exist they do. What we need to discuss is how to recognize and understand the way they exist. According to the teachings of the Nyingma tradition, we recognize phenomena to be the naturally arisen appearances of our mind. Such recognition acknowledges the Madhyamaka view that phenomena are established from karmic causes and conditions while at the same time, it accepts the Cittamatra view that external phenomena as the perception of our own mind. This is Maitreya Yogacara or Yogacara Madhyamaka.

Nyingma's acknowledgement of both the Madhyamaka and Cittamatrin positions, however, is not a middle-of-the-road compromise of the views of the two schools. Some contemporary scholars of Buddhism take the compound term literally and infer from it that Yogacara Madhyamaka is a hybrid of Cittamatra and Madhyamaka; others say that this cannot be so because the two views are irreconcilable. Considerable confusion results.

When phenomena naturally arise from the mind, there is no prejudice towards being either subjective (that is, not mind only) or objective (that is not matter only). This is the absolute truth that transcends dualistic concepts of mind and matter. If practitioners on the path to liberation focus primarily on mind, then their mind will become their constraint. If, on the other hand, they focus primarily on matter, then external phenomena will become their constraint. In neither of these two situations can the mind-itself be at ease. We must transcend the two in order to attain liberation.

Huineng's "mind that flutters" refers to the mind that naturally manifests. This is also "the flag that flutters" – the state of the mind become manifest. If practitioners wish to transcend all dualistic constraints and realize the true nature of all phenomena, they must go beyond mere intellectual understanding and gain actual experience of these states. This is the fundamental principle of the Great Madhyamaka and the Profound *Prajnaparamita*.

The bardo of *dharmata* is so named because it is the naturally arisen phenomena of the *dharmata*. Because of *vasana* or habitual tendencies, when the mental body is in the first stage of the bardo of *dharmata*, it recognizes phenomena that appear to be lights, flashes and noise. When the mental body enters the second stage, it not only experiences lights and so on, but also additional projections from its impure mind. In the first cycle of the second stage, the five poisons or *kleshas* (Skt. *klesha*) (greed, anger, delusion, jealousy and pride) are purified and transformed into the five peaceful deities. In the second cycle of the second stage, the peaceful deities are superseded by their wrathful counterparts. Each of the two cycles of the second stage is seven days long.

When the five poisons (greed, anger, ignorance, jealousy and pride) are naturally liberated, they become the five wisdoms. The Cittamatrins call this "transformation of the basis" (i.e. transforming the consciousness into wisdom). How then can our mind be transformed into wisdom? The Nyingma School adopts the method of *ldog pa*, a Tibetan term meaning to reverse, to go back. *Ldog pa* has four levels of meaning – outer, inner, secret and very secret. Here, we explain it only according to its outer meaning. For example, if we see a bottle before us, we consider it to be substantially existing and truly existing because of its appearance, based on our observation of its form and capabilities. However, when we realize its aspect of cognizance through our completion-stage practice, and realize its aspect of display through our generation-stage practice, and further realize the aspect of emptiness from its cognizance and display through the union of generation-stage and completion-stage practices, then what appears to us will be very different. After completing the three stages of practice, we will not recognize the bottle that naturally arises from our mind to be the same bottle as before, although there is still the appearance of a bottle in front of us. Prior to our realization, we identified the bottle as substantially and truly existing; but now, we recognize the emptiness of this naturally arisen "bottle" of the mind. In this way, the latter is said to be the *ldog pa* of the former. Similarly, we can see wisdom as the *ldog pa* of poisons. We can further understand that the wisdom symbolized by the peaceful and the wrathful deities is their *ldog pa*.

We need to understand that peaceful and wrathful deities only appear to the mind of a Buddhist practitioner's mental body. If the deceased followed another religion during his lifetime, the appearance arises in the form of the holy beings of that religion. For sentient beings who have less merit than humans, deities, be they peaceful or wrathful, do not appear. Instead, they see appearances that reflect their individual karma. We also need to understand that peaceful and wrathful are merely different mental actions. Through understanding this, we gain more insight into Huineng's statement "It is your mind that flutters."

Mental phenomena fall neither within the compass of the mind only view, as mere perceptions of our mind, nor within the subjective mind only view, as projections from our subjective mind. If we wish to understand both Chan Buddhism and the Great Madhyamaka, which have the same origin and share the same view, we should never interpret them from the perspective of the mind only or subjective mind only point of view. If we do, we will only distort the truth and fail to understand the path of meditation.

The nature of the mind, whether it is pure or impure, does not depend on concepts of mind only or matter only. A while ago, someone told me a joke that illustrates this statement. When they were up in space, American astronauts discovered that they could not use ballpoint pens in spacecraft because, without the force of gravity, the ink in the pen could not flow to the writing tip. American corporations immediately set about developing a pen that could be used in space. They spent two years and close to one billion US dollars doing so. Sometime later, American and Russian astronauts were collaborating on a project in space. The Americans were surprised that their Russian counterparts had pens to write with. They thought perhaps the Russians were as technologically advanced as the Americans. So they floated across the spacecraft to investigate. On looking closer they discovered that the Russians were actually using pencils! This is a funny example, but it illustrates quite clearly how easily obscured our mind can be. We become trapped by the concepts we are using. The Americans' idea was to have a ballpoint pen that astronauts could use to write in space. "Ballpoint pen" became a concept that obstructed their mind. The Russians had fewer resources; all they had in mind was something they could use to write with in space. The concept of a pen did not become an obstruction to their thinking process; neither did it distort their psychological response. So they simply used a pencil.

From this story, we can see that there is no need to involve the concepts of matter only or mind only. We can consider all phenomena to be the naturally arisen appearance of *dharmata* and consider the recognition of phenomena to be the naturally arisen appearance of the mind-itself. Although mind and consciousness are mentioned in the Nyingma teachings, this does not refer to the concept of mind only. The Nyingma school has solemnly affirmed that the statement "All phenomena are projections from the mind" is not the definitive meaning of the truth because it focuses too much on the true existence of the mind.

In the *Bardo Thodol,* the guided instructions for the bardo being upon commencement of the first stage of lights, flashes and noise are as follows. "Do not be frightened by the appearance of the bardo of *dharmata.* All these phenomena in the bardo are mere appearances arising from your mind." (This section of the instructions is based on the Cittamatrin view). The instructions continue,

> "Virtuous man. When your mind is separated from your physical body, the subtle drop of *dharmata*, pure, lucent and radiant, is in the nature of a dazzling glow, so bright that it may intimidate you. Like the glistening reflection of a blazing sun on serene waters, it glitters with shimmering pearls of brightness. Please do not be frightened. It is your primordial clear light of *dharmata*." (This step goes beyond that of the Cittamatrins).

Besides naturally arisen form, there is also naturally arisen sound. The instructions continue,

> "In this clear light is the primordial sound of the *dharmata*. It is deafeningly loud, like the striking of a thousand thunderclaps. However, this roaring sound of thunder is merely your primordial sound of *dharmata*. There is no need to feel panic or fear."

According to the Great Madhyamaka, everything including form, sound, smell, taste and touch is mere naturally arisen phenomena. Because they are naturally arisen, they have no inherent existence. Therefore, phenomena can manifest to different environments adaptively. For example, during our lifetime, the luminous subtle drop of *dharmata* does not manifest as a terrifying, blazing light. However, in the bardo, its manifestation will threaten the mental body in the bardo of *dharmata*. This is an example of adaptation. During our lifetime, we will never hear our primordial sound of *dharmata*; however, to the mental body in the bardo, it roars like a thousand claps of thunder. This is another example of adapting to the different constraints of the domain of existence. Theoretically, the mental body should also experience terrifying smells tastes and touch. However, forms and sounds impose the greatest threat to the mental body of bardo of *dharmata* because they are the main objects of our habitual tendencies during our lifetime. Our eyes and ears are more sensitive than our other sense organs. That is why the experience of the latter senses is not mentioned.

The instruction continues:

The mental body you now possess is different from the physical body you have during your lifetime. No matter how terrifying the sounds, light and flashes appear, they cannot harm you and cannot cause you to die. Just recognize that they are the manifestations of your own mind. That will be sufficient. If you cannot recognize that these phenomena are mere manifestations of your own mind, no matter how diligently you have practised during your lifetime, you will be terrified by the blazing light, shocked by the piercing flashes and frightened by the pounding sounds. If you do not understand the key points of this teaching and cannot recognize the true nature of the sound, light and flashes, you will once again have to fall back into samsaric cyclic existence.

According to the special meaning in the Great Madhyamaka of the Nyingma tradition, we can attain natural liberation if we recognize phenomena as naturally arising. We have already discussed this in previous chapters. If we take the view of either Cittamatra only or Madhyamaka only to explain how liberation is attained in the bardo, it will be very difficult to clarify how recognizing lights, flashes and noise as manifestations of our own mind can lead to liberation from samsaric cyclic existence. In the bardo of *dharmata*, we cannot attain liberation unless we recognize that all phenomena – sound, light and flashes, as well as peaceful and wrathful deities – are mere natural-arisen phenomena of the mind. We must also realize that all these phenomena are the natural manifestations of the *dharmata* recognized as the naturally arisen phenomena of the mind-itself. In this way, we realize its *ldog pa*. After realizing its *ldog pa,* our mind transforms into wisdom. This is what Maitreya Yogacara calls transformation, and what Chan Buddhism describes as original face. According to the Great Madhyamaka, it is natural liberation.

CHAPTER 18

The Bardo of *Dharmata* (Part 2)

The Arising of The Four Visions

THE PURPOSE OF PRACTICING the bardo of *dharmata* is to evoke four successive visions: the vision of direct realization of the ultimate nature; the vision of the increase of experience; the vision of the perfection of intrinsic awareness; and the vision of cessation into the ultimate nature (*dharmata*). There is a verse about the four visions:

> Due to the realization of the ultimate nature,
>   attachment to external phenomena ceases.
> Due to increasing experience,
>   primordial wisdom arises.
> Due to the perfection of intrinsic awareness,
>   the *Sambhogakaya* is recognized.
> Due to the cessation into the ultimate nature,
>   the great perfection is spontaneously realized.

The above verse summarizes the progressive stages of realization, based on the four visionary displays of the meditation of leap-over (Tib. *thod rgal*). Although attaining the second stage – the vision of the increase of experience – does not imply liberation in our lifetime, it is still regarded as an important practice of the six bardos. This is because, if we have attained such a realization during this lifetime, it is almost certain that we will attain liberation in the bardo state after death. Since it is difficult for most of us to attain liberation during our lifetime, this practice of ensuring liberation upon our death therefore assumes greater importance.

Those who have no training in these four visions may find them rather cryptic and difficult to realize. Sometimes, even when we practise diligently, no substantive results in terms of insights are seen. Those who are not confident in this practice must rely on the transference of consciousness to attain liberation in the bardo of dying instead of relying on the practices of the bardo of dharmata. Once the consciousness of the deceased reaches the bardo of dharmata, before liberation is possible, it must at least be able to recognize what visionary displays are. That is why practices relating to the bardo of dharmata are so important. Because of this, we shall now explain these four visions in more detail.

The Vision of Direct Realization of Ultimate Nature

As discussed before, visionary displays do not refer to mere appearances seen by the eyes or to sounds heard by the ears. They are the vital dynamics orchestrated by sounds or appearances and the liveliness expressed within. Some practitioners think that the noise and bustle of society is an impediment to their spiritual practice and so they withdraw to a secluded mountain, trying to isolate themselves from all the distractions of the mundane world. Such a retreat can be conducive to certain stages of our practice. We should be aware, however, that even the quietest hillside is not completely motionless or distraction-free. Even if we hide ourselves deep in the mountain, the dynamics of the trees and the sky are still readily observable. We can still be distracted by chirping birds and buzzing bees, or by beautiful eye-catching flowers. It is not necessary, therefore, to find an absolutely silent, motionless environment in which to practise. Wherever there is life, there are dynamic forces in action. We should not try to avoid them, but rather we should recognize them with increasing clarity as we advance in our *samadhi*.

Among the eight divisions of *samadhi* mentioned in the *Abhidharma-kosa-sastra*, four divisions are in the form realm, and four are in the formless realm. Of the four *samadhi* in the form realm, the highest state is called the *samadhi* of the four *devalokas*, a state in which all feelings for worldly pleasure are renounced. In this state, the mind is like a clear polished mirror, free from the tiniest speck of dust. Yet even in this highest state of stillness, there are countless phenomena appearing. It is not a void. In the four divisions of *samadhi* in the formless realm, even though the forms of the material world are not objects of meditation, the *samadhi* is not separate from liveliness. The progressive levels of *samadhi* are attained by first meditating on the emptiness of space and then meditating on the mind (the mind is certainly teeming with aliveness). When we have transcended the mind, meditation becomes non-referential. As we progress even further, we enter a state of complete purity, beyond appearance and non-appearance. Even though the meditation is non-referential, however, it is not separate from liveliness. The state beyond appearance and non-appearance is a state that is not separate from all phenomenal expressions; neither is it attached to them.

As the vitality of the *dharmadhatu* does not cease, so also its dynamics do not cease. No matter how subtle the movement or vibration, it is still a part of this liveliness. The state of outermost stillness is merely a state of the subtlest dynamics – not a complete cessation of it. If there were no dynamic forces in action, we would fall into a state of nothingness, the state of nihilistic emptiness about which Buddha Shakyamuni warned. In the *Maharatnakuta Sutra*, Buddha Sakyamuni said to his disciple, "Ananda, I would rather see people grasping onto me, and holding me higher than Mount Meru, than seeing people grasping onto emptiness and considering it the same as nothingness." Why did he say this? Because, while self-grasping can be eliminated through directly realizing emptiness, there is no antidote whatsoever to grasping onto nothingness. There is no available remedy because the vitality in the mind has already perished, and everything appears lifeless. This is not a desirable state of *samadhi* of non-referential meditation, but rather a state of listlessness resulting from seeing the objects of meditation as dead objects.

Everything is alive in *dharmadhatu*. Someone may ask, "Is there life in a piece of cold hard rock?" We can answer, "Yes. If you examine that cold rock even casually, you can feel its living energy from its intrinsic qualities and rhythmic patterns." Once we feel its vitality, the dynamism within it becomes apparent. Therefore, in the vision of direct realization of the ultimate nature, whether our *samadhi* is with form or without form, the vitality that pervades our mind and the environment never ceases. Furthermore, its presence constantly manifests itself, even if, in our generation-stage meditation, we are generating a static image of our personal deity and his or her *mandala*. The most important thing is to infuse the visualization with vitality. This does not mean that our personal deity in the *mandala* has to walk and talk in a mundane sense. But it is important for us to recognize the personal deity is an actual being, full of life and creativity. Even the lotus seat on which he or she sits should be seen as a real lotus; we should be able to feel the satiny texture of the petals and appreciate their colours. In our meditation, we want to generate a warm and lively presence of our deity and his or her *mandala*.

Although the vision of direct realization of the ultimate nature is not a generation-stage practice of visualizing the personal deity and his or her *mandala*, it still employs clear light in presenting its meaning. This luminous state is not only lucent and clear, but also dynamic and alive. As described in the *Tantra of Natural-Manifestation of Luminous Rigpa* (Tib. *Rig pa rang shar*):

These luminous forms possess the five wisdoms
Resplendently expressed as the *vajra* chains
Constantly approaching and departing
Suddenly darting, suddenly amassing

From this verse, we can see that the vision of direct realization of the ultimate nature is neither separate from nor one with our primordial awareness, *rigpa*. We cannot say that *rigpa* is either the same as or different to the vision of direct realization of the ultimate nature. Let's take the analogy of the sun and its rays as an example. The rays radiate, and although they are never separate from the sun, neither are they the same as it. In this practice, the expanse of luminosity is the mark of *dharmata*. A tiny, luminous drop, the size of a mustard seed, appears within this luminosity. It is the mark of primordial wisdom. Inside the luminous drop there is a slender *vajra* chain. It is the mark of *rigpa* and its creative embodiment. This state experienced by the practitioner is the vision of the ultimate nature of *rigpa* manifested in space.

The Vision of the Increase of Experience

As previously discussed, there are countless naturally arisen phenomena in the fathomless *dharmadhatu*. We hypothesize a base, called primordial ground, from which all these phenomena naturally arise. Within the limits of our mind, however, we cannot recognize the naturally arisen displays of *dharmadhatu*. Our understanding is limited to the world we experience through our sensory powers.

Under this hypothesis, naturally arisen phenomena can be divided into those of the *dharmata* and those of the mind-itself. The naturally arisen phenomena of the *dharmata* transcend the constraints of time and space, while those of the mind-itself fall within those constraints. Hence, the former encompass the latter. This then gives rise to the question: how do we recognize and transcend the naturally arisen phenomena within the constraints of time and space of our phenomenal world, and progress to the next step of recognizing the naturally arisen phenomena of *dharmata*, which are free from such constraints? The practices of recognizing these four visions have been established to address this particular question. Some may wonder whether realizing the first stage – the vision of direct realization of the ultimate nature – would enable us to transcend time and space and recognize the vision of the naturally arisen displays of the ultimate nature, the *dharmata*. To answer this question, we have to start from the beginning.

The concepts of naturally arisen phenomena of *dharmata* and naturally arisen phenomena of the mind-itself are established as a means to transcend our grasping onto true existence. Most people misunderstand the concept of naturally arising and mistake the phenomena that arise as truly existing externally to the mind. As a result, the I and the external phenomena become two separate, opposing entities. From this innate delusion, phenomena appear to be solid and real, and so does our I. Consequently, most people hold the so-called naturally arising phenomena of the empty ground to be substantially existing "things." As a result, the mind recognizes all phenomena and concepts to exist in a very real and tangible sense; even the mind is regarded as truly existing in the same way. Because of this, numerous methods have been developed to help us transcend this innate grasping onto existence. Cittamatrin and Madhyamaka are two of the schools of thought established to transcend this innate delusion. The concept of naturally arising falls under the aegis of Madhyamaka philosophy, which can be further divided into Outer and Inner Madhyamaka. When the nature of naturally arisen phenomena is realized through the concept of dependent relationships, this is Outer Madhyamaka. It is so called because the concept of dependent relationships is based on the concept of phenomena, or things external to us. On the other hand, when the empty nature of naturally arisen phenomena is realized through their cognizance and infinite displays, and these three aspects are further realized not to be different from each other, we call this Inner Madhyamaka. It is called Inner Madhyamaka because no external concepts are imposed over or above it. We realize absolute truth through realizing the inseparability of the three aspects. Inner Madhyamaka is also called Great Madhyamaka. In actuality, it is Maitreya Yogacara. It does not contradict Nagarjuna's view of emptiness based on dependent arising.

Within the naturally arisen displays of *dharmata*, phenomena in samsara also arise naturally but are subject to the law of dependent relationships. Since we are in samsara, all phenomena we encounter must therefore also be dependently related. From this, we can see that the Great Madhyamaka, which is established to realize the state of naturally arisen display, does not contradict the law of dependent arising. The uniqueness of this approach is to realize emptiness spontaneously without contriving any additional concepts of emptiness of phenomena. When we abide in this natural uncontrived state, the three natures of dependent arising will automatically be transcended.

The term the three natures of dependent arising (Tib. *Rten 'brel gyi rang bzhin gsum*) refers to the threefold dependent arising that falls within the limits of the mind. The three natures are karma and causality (Tib. *phrad*), relativity (Tib. *ltos*) and mutual dependency (Tib. *rten*). When we use the threefold dependent arising relationship to observe phenomena, eventually we will realize the *ldog pa* (reverse) of phenomena, and hence transcend our mind. At that time, however, we are in fact within the bounds of the dependent arising of mutual obstruction. In order to transcend it, we have to realize how to go beyond the constraints of time and space, and those imposed by our mind while subject to the same constraints. When we have transcended this final layer of constraints, we will be free from all obstructions.

The key to realizing emptiness is, in fact, rather simple. What we need to understand is that all contrived thoughts are fabricated concepts over and above the nature of things. If we want to realize emptiness spontaneously, we have to rest our mind in its natural pure state, free of any contrivances or elaborations. In our daily lives, we do not need to emphasize that we are using the emptiness of water to shower, or drinking the emptiness of water to slake our thirst. Similarly we do not need to stare at the water to contemplate that it arises dependent on cause and conditions in order to conclude that its nature is empty. If we do that, we are pasting concepts over and above the water. What we should do is recognize the aspects of cognizance and infinite displays in our daily life. Then we would realize that water is, in fact, a naturally arisen phenomenon of our mind-itself. In this way, not only would we realize that the nature of water is empty, but we would realize that water is the naturally arisen display of *dharmata* composed of its three inseparable aspects – emptiness, cognizance and infinite displays, not separate from each other. When these three aspects – cognizance, emptiness and infinite displays – spontaneously dissolve, what remains is the state of our own inner realization. This is why Chan Buddhism places so much emphasis on observing our daily chores. I recall a Chan story:

> After serving his Chan master for ten years, a young novice be-
> came a monk. Throughout this time, he wondered why his teacher
> had not given him any teachings. He could not stop thinking
> about it. So one day he decided to ask his teacher directly.
> "Master, could you teach me how to practise Chan?" On hearing
> the question, the Chan master slapped the boy's face. He replied,
> "In these ten years, you brewed the tea and I drank it; you boiled
> the rice and I ate it. And you say I have not taught you how to
> practise Chan?"

Observing our daily chores with what Chan Buddhism refers to as ordinary mind as a means to recognizing naturally arisen displays can bring peace to the mind-itself, but not liberation. When one has not transcended the boundaries of time and space, the mind-itself is constrained to recognize all phenomena as the naturally arisen display of the mind-itself. The vision of the ultimate nature so recognized is merely the vision of the mind-itself. The vision of the naturally arisen display of mind-itself is labelled as the vision of the ultimate nature in name only.

Now, to qualify as an increase of experience, the scope of our attainment has to be increased – beyond the dimension of time and space. When we can achieve that state, we have then realized the visionary displays of direct realization of the ultimate nature. At that point, we attain the natural liberation of the mind-itself and simultaneously abide in the *dharmata*. What is the vision of the increase of experience? How does the practitioner transcend time and space? Human beings have only one tool to transcend time and space: clear light (its luminosity, not the light itself). This clear light is, in fact, an inherent capability of the mind. We call it the clear light of mind. This clear light of mind can transcend time; through it, we can travel back in time to visit the past or go forward to visit the future. It can also transcend space, allowing us to travel instantaneously from Fifth Avenue in Manhattan to the Leaning Tower of Pisa in Italy. (It hasn't yet transcended the three-dimensional domain.) We can only transcend the constraints of our phenomenal world through the clear light of mind. Through practice, we will attain an increase of experience. Eventually, our experience will increase to a state that enables us to abide in *dharmata*, a state beyond the limits of time and space. This is described in the root text of the six bardos. When there is an increase of experience, the *rigpa*, primordial awareness, first becomes like a bird ready to soar, then like a wild deer running, then like a bee hovering over honey. These are akin to the increasingly effortless states of mind experienced when breaking the boundary of time and space. Lastly, *rigpa* is described to be in perfect stillness, meaning that it has abided in *dharmata*. This is called the displayed wisdom of *rigpa* in the bardo, or the clear light of the wisdom of *rigpa*. Why do we call this state the displayed wisdom of *rigpa* in the bardo? In the two seven-day cycles of the bardo of *dharmata*, peaceful and wrathful deities appear to the consciousness of the deceased. Such appearances are the mere visionary displays of *dharmata* that arise naturally. When the consciousness of the deceased recognizes the vision of direct realization of the ultimate nature, and has thus attained an increase of experience, this experience is the wisdom of *rigpa* in the bardo.

The Vision of the Perfection of Intrinsic Awareness

As the visions develop, the embodiments of the five Buddha families together with their consorts will appear in a *vajra* state in each luminous drop. An immeasurable number of them appear, filling the field of vision, pervading every pore of the skin. This merely describes the appearance of the vision, however, and not the realization. To describe its related realization can be a rather involved task. In simplified terms, the practitioner has realized the primordial ground. From the perspective of the mind-itself, *tathagatagarbha* has been realized. As previously discussed, the primordial ground is the basis for all naturally arisen displays of *dharmata* in the *dharmadhatu*, whereas *tathagatagarbha* is the basis for all pure, lucent displays of the mind-itself. Primordial ground and *tathagatagarbha* are similar to a spotless mirror. When it is dirtied, the primordial ground becomes the constrained domain – such as the dimensions of time and space – upon which the phenomenal world depends, and *tathagatagarbha* becomes *alayavijnana*. The goal of our practices is to transcend *alayavijnana* to realize *tathagatagarbha* and also to transcend the dimension of time and space which our phenomena world depends upon to realize primordial ground. In other words, we have to realize a spotless mirror from which all phenomena arise. Normally, we can only see images in a mirror because we, too, are inside the mirror. If we escape from the mirror, we instantly recognize that those images as mere reflections and that the mirror is the basis for all these naturally arisen appearances. The experience of realizing *tathagatagarbha*, or primordial ground, is difficult to articulate in words. We can only call it the natural liberation of *dharmata*, a state of inconceivability.

The Vision of Cessation into Ultimate Nature

We will discuss this topic only briefly. It can be compared to the new moon phase of the lunar cycle. We cannot see the moon at that time, but this does not mean there is no moon. In other words, the naturally arisen display of the *dharmata* of the moon is always there. We cannot equate a new moon with a full moon because in the former case the moon does not appear, while in the latter case the moon appears full and round. As a result, we lose equanimity. This lack of equanimity in our observation is a big obstacle to liberation. It can hinder us from transcending the constraints of time and space. We cannot conceive existence in two-dimensional domains or four-dimensional domains. Therefore, we assume that sentient beings exist only in three-dimensional form, just as we only recognize the moon when we can see it shining in the sky. The vision of cessation into the ultimate nature is analogous to a state in which we can transcend the limits imposed by our mind and realize that the new moon actually exists and is as solid and round as the full moon. Only in this way can we realize the vitality (the aspect of infinite displays) that is omnipresent and pervades all dimensions, the whole *dharmadhatu*. From this vitality, we can then spontaneously recognize the naturally arisen displays of *dharmata*.

The visionary displays that we realize at this stage are beyond form body and sensory perceptions, and also beyond our phenomenal world. The state of inconceivability is beyond conception, beyond all words and elaborations. It abides neither in the mind-itself nor in *dharmata*. In the ultimate state, it does not abide in equanimity. We call this the natural liberation of equanimity.

Let's give a brief summary of the four visions. They are:

> The vision of direct realization of the ultimate nature,
>   which abides in the mind-itself.
> The vision of the increase of experience, abides in
>   *dharmata*(natural liberation of the mind-itself).
> The vision of the perfection of intrinsic awareness, which
>   abides in equanimity (natural liberation of *dharmata*).
> The vision of cessation into the ultimate nature, which
>   abides in natural liberation of equanimity.

This is the training of bodhisattvas, from the second ground up to Buddhahood. The Nyingma tradition has instructions for every stage of practice. In each stage, there are marks that reflect our attainments. It is not appropriate to introduce detailed instructions here because to practise, we must rely on the guidance of a guru. Daily practice is of prime importance.

Regarding realizations, it is also inappropriate to elaborate on them here. Once a realization is mentioned, it becomes a concept on to which practitioners hold fast. Having a preconceived idea of how a certain state of realization should be actually hinders it from arising spontaneously. Like tasting water, only the person drinking it can really tell how it tastes. If we were to create a subjective concept of how water should taste, it would only hinder the person who is drinking the water to fully experience the flavour of it.

CHAPTER 19

The Bardo of Becoming (Part 1)

Mental Body and Body of Habitual Tendencies

THE LAST BARDO OF THE SIX BARDOS is called the bardo of becoming or existence (Tib. *srid pa bardo*). The practice is described as opening up a blocked water channel by joining it with another channel. The bardo of becoming is the stage leading to the event of rebirth. Some religions repudiate the doctrine of reincarnation. If we look closer at the issues involved, the disagreements are mostly related to the type of rebirth that brings about a conception in the womb. Not all rebirths, however, have to take place in a womb. If we explain that rebirths can be in an emanated form of gods and goddesses, perhaps some may look at the whole matter differently. In Hinduism, for example, some followers believe that sentient beings live many lives until they attain perfection and become one with the Divine.

The idea of rebirth or "becoming a form of existence" in Buddhism is distinguished from other religions in many ways. In the Buddhist view, rebirth is not a continuation of the individual self of the deceased. When John or Jane dies, it is not his or her individual soul, still possessing the same character, that carries on to the next life. Someone may then ask, "Buddhists say a bardo body exists. If a bardo being is not a soul, what is it?" We would answer, "A bardo being is a merely a state of mind carrying the karma accumulated since beginning-less time. It does not exist in any particular form. This state of mind carries the mental force of the deceased, which forms a mental body. The mental body does not last very long. As time passes, it will turn into a body of habitual tendencies. We have these habitual tendencies throughout the course of our life; for example, the I that we see in our dreams is our body of habitual tendencies. At the moment of death, habitual tendencies are inactive; that is why the best opportunity to attain liberation is during the two manifestations of clear light of death. The mental body in the initial stage of the bardo is essentially free from thoughts that are connected with the deceased's habitual tendencies; for this reason, it is also called pure illusory body."

The emergence of the body of habitual tendencies is easily triggered. When the mental body hears its family members cry or sees its favorite belongings, its habitual tendencies will take effect. It will gradually increases in strength and take over the mental body. This form of illusory body is no longer pure. Since it is propelled by its habitual tendencies, it will take on the form of its immediate past life along with the characteristics of its next life (the realm in which it will take rebirth). We call this form "the body of past and emergent life." The bardo being will also see scenes related to its emergent life. Neither the mental body nor the body of habitual tendencies is what we call think of as a soul or spirit. This is especially obvious for the body of habitual tendencies that contains the habitual tendencies from countless lives. When the habitual tendencies take effect, we cannot ascertain in which life they were formed.

Someone may ask, "If the I that we see in our dreams is the body of habitual tendencies, then the body of habitual tendencies must be together with our physical body. Why then do we identify ourselves as I while the body of habitual tendencies cannot be identified as such?" We can answer it this way: "We are different from the mental body because we have a physical body made of blood and flesh. This physical body, which so convincingly appears to exist inherently, becomes the emblem of the I with which we identify. The mental body, however, is merely an illusory appearance that embodies the consciousness of the deceased. It loses the emblematic quality of an I identified with a body made of flesh and blood. When the habitual tendencies intensify, meaning that the throwing force of karma intensifies, the consciousness of the deceased will no longer able to maintain the same appearance of the mental body. It cannot give the mental body a constant identity, as it would if the mental body were someone's individual soul or spirit."

The main reason we grasp onto the I and mark it as a distinct separate identity is that we have a physical body. When the consciousness is separated from the body, the I loses its firmly grounded identity. Because of this, rebirth is construed by Buddhists to be the passing of a collection of karma from one form into another. It neither perpetuates nor interrupts a fixed identity like a spirit or soul. The collection of karma continues; since it does not undergo a discontinuation, it is not interrupting. The not-perpetuating and not-interrupting nature of rebirth is likened to lighting a new candle with the dying flame of an old candle. It is not-perpetuating in the sense that the flame is not burning from the same candle; it is not-interrupting as the candle flame continues to burn.

Our cyclic existence in samsara is just like that. The collection of karma takes on a new body, and this new body initiates actions that accumulate new karma. When the body dies, the accumulated karma once again finds a new body. This cycle of rebirth repeats itself again and again. We cannot say that there is a fixed identity in taking rebirth, yet there is the karma accumulated by an identity.

This detailed explanation will enable us to understand easily how to attain liberation in the bardo of becoming. When liberation is attained, the entire collection of karma, and not an entity such as a prisoner, is liberated. This mental body of habitual tendencies is described in the tantras as the body of past and emergent life:

> The bodily form of past and emergent lives
> Complete with unobstructed senses,
> Endowed with clairvoyance and miraculous abilities,
> Derived from the past actions,
> Through the clairvoyance of divine eyes,
> It sees other bardo beings similar in kind.

It is interesting to note that the emergence of this bodily form is not related to our spiritual beliefs. Whether or not the deceased believed in rebirth, through its imagination, his or her consciousness can embody a form. This body is not a physical body but a vision that resembles the physical body of the deceased but without flesh and blood. It is like the bodily forms we see in our dreams. Unless we deny the appearance of bodily forms in dreams, we cannot deny the appearance of the mental body of habitual tendencies. In a dream, we do not have full control in the way we appear. We cannot merely choose how we appear in our dreams. Sometimes, our appearance changes in the middle of a dream. We can suddenly get old, or young; our body can grow to the size of a mountain, or shrink to the size of an ant. How can this happen? It happens because appearances in our dreams are directed by our habitual tendencies, and not entirely controlled by our consciousness.

In fact, we should be very familiar with the bodily form of our mental body in the bardo because it is just like our I appearing in a dream. Generally speaking, when our mental body first emerges in the bardo, it takes on the appearance of ourselves looking our best. No matter how gaunt we looked before we died, our mental body will look young and beautiful. No matter how poor and shabby we looked the moment we died, our mental body will appear affluent and well-dressed. This is because the consciousness of the deceased embellishes the bodily form with its best appearance from its past life. This perfect bodily form will last three-and-a-half days (that is, three-and-a-half days after the two seven-day cycles of the appearance of the peaceful and wrathful deities). After this three-and-a half-day period, the habitual tendencies propelled by our karma start to make their influence felt. This is inevitable because the mental body carries the karma of countless lives, some of which will inevitably take effect. This includes the effect of previous actions propelled by greed, anger, ignorance, jealously and pride. They reinforce each other, like a chain of causes, actions and effects that repeats itself again and again, in an endless cycle. During our life, one karmic action causes another. A later action reinforces the effect of an earlier one. Karmic causes, actions and effects get tangled in a maze of intertwining nets. In this way, the influence of habitual tendencies infiltrates into the mental body.

Habitual tendencies affect the process of rebirth in the following two ways. First, they have a direct effect on the bardo being, compelling it to take rebirth in one of the six realms. Second, whatever the realm, habitual tendencies produce an environmental effect that determines the conditions of the particular environment in which the bardo being takes rebirth. The most powerful action determines the direct effect; other actions determine the environmental effects. In the bardo of becoming, the body of habitual tendencies will come to experience both effects before it takes rebirth. It will see scenes relating to one of the six realms and the conditions of the environment. The mental body will also exhibit the signs and characteristics of its emerging form of existence. For example, if it is to be reborn into a monkey, it will start scrambling about; if it will be reborn in the realm of the demi-gods, it will start being antagonistic. This is what the form body of past and emergent life means. The bodily form referred to is not its physical body (the body of flesh and blood), but a form body. This form body is often referred to as the subtle body: its form is influenced by the consciousness of its immediate past life and the conditions of the emergent life.

The next description, "complete with unobstructed senses," means that the mental body is complete with perfect sense faculties (eye, ear, nose, tongue, body and consciousness). It does not matter if any of these sense faculties were impaired while the bardo being was living; they function perfectly in the mental body of the bardo. The blind are now able to see, and the deaf to hear. Furthermore, the mental body can hear from whomever it wants within its karmic perimeter; it can travel anywhere in the world to hear from a close friend. Its faultless sense faculties give rise to powerful clairvoyance. Yet, despite the strength of its sense faculties, the mental body cannot exceed the boundary of its karmic disposition.

The third description, "Endowed with clairvoyance and miraculous abilities derived from past actions," refers to the karmically produced abilities the mental body possesses: clairvoyance such as divine eyes and divine ears, the ability to pass unimpeded through solid matter like walls and rocks, and the ability to arrive anywhere instantly just by thinking about the place (so long as it is within its karmic boundary). We must not be excited about possessing these miraculous abilities, however, because they are neither *siddhis* (Tib. *dngos grub*) (accomplishments) resulting from Dharma practice nor the fruit of meditative stabilization. They are merely the result of karma. They are result of the power consciousness having broken away from the fetters of the physical body. Bardo beings should not use theses abilities if it is not absolutely necessary because, every time they are used, they have to be directed by the consciousness, and every time the consciousness directs an action, the action becomes the cause of future effects. This cumulative karma further entangles the maze of intertwining karmic net, making liberation increasingly difficult.

At this point, we should know that once the consciousness has embodied a bodily form, the best opportunity for it to attain liberation is in the two seven-day cycles of the bardo of *dharmata*. The next best time is the first three-an-a-half-day cycle of the bardo of becoming. Once the body of habitual tendencies takes shape, it is approaching the stage of rebirth.

The last description says, "Through the clairvoyance of divine eyes, it sees other bardo beings similar in kind." As mentioned earlier, such clairvoyance cannot be attributed to our attainments on the spiritual path. It is merely an attribute of the mental body of the bardo. Through concentration, the mental body will see gods and goddesses if it will take rebirth in the god realm; it will see humans if it will take rebirth in the human realm, and so on. Some mental bodies in the bardo can communicate with the mental body of humans. To the living person, the deceased appears in his dream. To bardo being, to communicate with the living person is to meet with the mental body of the living person through entering his dream. If the mental body of the bardo takes rebirth in the other five realms, it then will not be able to see any humans.

Knowing that the mental body of the bardo has such miraculous powers, some may think that the bardo being must be remarkably free. In actuality, the mental body is not that free. Once it loses its physical body, it feels that it has nothing on which to hold. Sometimes, the whole body feels as if it has melted and disintegrated. Fear arises. This fear evokes terrifying scenes of the six realms. Even the bardo being who is to be reborn in the god realm feels fear.

The guided instructions in *Natural Liberation* describe the mental bodies of the bardo:

> You roam and rove
> Because of the karmic wind
> Never can you obtain any rest
> Your mind has nothing to depend on
> Like the bird's feather being blown off by the wind
> Like a rider on horse of wind,
> Always wafting, never resting.

If we imagine how exhausting the life of a fugitive who is endlessly running must be, we can easily understand why the mental body of the bardo yearns to take rebirth. The bardo being is desperate for a shelter, a physical body, a place for refuge (such as a womb). After being in the bardo of *dharmata*, the bardo being is in the bardo of becoming from anywhere from one week up to seven weeks depending on its karma and on which realm it will take rebirth. Generally speaking, it is in the bardo for three to four weeks. After that, the moment of rebirth arrives. As mentioned earlier, the kind of rebirth a bardo being takes is determined by the direct effect and environmental effect of its actions. If both direct effect and environmental effect are superior, it takes rebirth in the god realm; if the direct effect is not as good, it takes rebirth in the demi-god or human realm. If it is born in the human realm with good environmental effect, it takes rebirth in a hospitable place where both material resources and spiritual comfort are available. If the direct effect is good and environmental effect is not, then it takes rebirth in any one of the three higher realms (gods, demi-gods, and human). The condition of the environment that it experiences depends on its karma. Take the example of a being born in a war-torn or impoverished country. Although he is reborn as a human (good direct effect), he constantly has to face hunger and other deprivations, and live without spiritual or material comfort. If the direct effect is not good but environmental effect is, then the bardo being takes rebirth in one of the lower three realms (animal, hungry ghost, and hell), but experiences an environment far superior to that of its peers. For example, it could be reborn in the animal realm, but as a pampered pet. If both direct effect and environmental effect are not good, then the bardo being will be compelled to take rebirth in the lower three realms and experience an environment worse than its peers. For example, it could be reborn as a starving stray dog.

Since the mental body of the bardo is endowed with the attributes of both its immediate past and emergent lives, before taking rebirth it can feel the two effects of its past actions. If its emergent life does not look promising, fear will arise. The fear causes pain. In a vicious cycle, this pain provokes further actions that in turn cause more pain. At this stage, the bardo being feels very lonely and helpless. For this reason, instructions on how to deal with the bardo of becoming are indispensable.

Before we explain the instructions on the bardo of becoming in more detail, let us understand the more about the scenes related to the six realms. According to the tantras, scenes of hurricanes often appear in the bardo. The bardo being can hear the sound of raging wind and crashing waves. It can also hear earth cracking and mountains crumbling. The worse its karma, the more terrifying the sounds. Moreover, hostile beings often appear. How frightening they appear to the bardo being depends on its karma. The hostile beings may be carrying weapons and howling to kill. Some bardo beings see themselves chased by voracious beasts; others see themselves in dense unfathomable darkness, like the dark before the arrival of a thunderstorm. The frightening visions pressure the bardo being into fleeing to a shelter. In the beginning, it manages to stabilize itself by holding onto Buddha statues, pagodas, temples, bridges, or even big trees, large rocks and the like. However, unless the bardo being was trained in meditative stabilization while it was in its previous life (not necessarily Buddhist meditative absorption; other forms of meditative stabilization are possible), it will not be able to stabilize itself when the body of habitual tendencies has completely taken shape. At that time, the bardo being sees the realm in which it will soon take rebirth.

If the bardo being is to take rebirth in the god realm, it sees celestial palaces made of jewels, so exquisite they are beyond our imagination. Even the roads are paved with gold, and the lawns are dotted with precious stones. All these are illusions. Those who do not regard gold and precious stones as special see different forms. Whatever forms they see, they are exquisite. To one who is not seeking liberation, this is a comfortable place of refuge. For those who seek liberation, however, the god realm is a dangerous place. The bardo being carries not only positive karma but also negative. Being reborn in a god realm means a life of ease; this is the result of the ripening of positive karma. However, ripening also means depleting. If positive karma is depleted to the extent that negative karma comes into play, then, unless the bardo being can attain liberation, it can easily be drawn to a lower rebirth. In the course of our life, we may have met people who are intelligent and honest but yet have to endure a life of poverty and social contempt. They are people who had a good direct effect but were deficient in the environmental effect; possibly they have been reborn from the god realm. According to the sutras, there are gods and goddesses who have reborn as hungry ghosts and hell beings. For those who seek liberation, the god realm is not a realm to which they should aspire.

If the bardo being is to take rebirth in the demi-god realm, it sees palaces and gardens but at the same time it also sees whirling wheels of fire. We must not aspire to be reborn in such realm. Demi-gods have a mind of intense hatred. Their minds are constantly focused on combat and war, and they can always find reasons to start one. Furthermore, if we are reborn in the realm of demi-gods, although there are many pleasures to be enjoyed, it is extremely easy to fall into the hell realm in the next rebirth.

If the bardo being takes rebirth in human realm, it sees the scene of the four continents. In the east is the continent Pervavideha, where there is a lake with swans and geese. In the west is Aparagodaniya, where there is a lake with horses around its shores. In the north is the continent Uttarakuru, where there is a lake with cattle or trees around its shores. It should be noted in these three continents, Buddhist teachings are not promulgated. Those who seek enlightenment should never wander there. Only the continent in the south, Jampudvipa, has Buddhist teachings. There are beautiful houses and grand mansions (not celestial temples). If the bardo being wants to take rebirth in such a realm, it should settle there and wait for the time to come.

A bardo being should never settle in the three lower realms. If it is to take rebirth in the animal realm, it sees rocks, caves and small houses covered with smoke. For the hungry ghost realm, it sees tree stumps, steep cliffs, desolate gorges and decayed woodlands, all filled with total darkness. For the hell realm, it sees dark lands where there are black iron houses, houses as red as blood, dark earth pits and dark roads. There is also music of bad karma, which sounds attractive to those with similar karma. No one can prove these scenarios of the emergent life. Whether we really believe in them or not is not important. What matters is that we understand them; understanding the teachings only brings benefits, not harm.

CHAPTER 20

The Bardo of Becoming (Part 2)

Six Ways of Blocking the Entrance of the Womb

THE MAIN TEACHING OF THE BARDO OF BECOMING concerns blocking the entrance of the womb. There are six methods for doing this:

> With one's personal deity;
> With one's spiritual guru and his consort;
> By generating the four states of bliss;
> With the antidote of renunciation;
> With the clear light of purity;
> With the illusory body.

These six ways of blocking the entrance of the womb are not restricted to any particular religion; however, without faith, it will be difficult to achieve the desired result in the bardo of becoming. In order to be successful in blocking the entrance of the womb, some methods require commitment to a regular practice during our lifetime. Because of this requirement, the practice instructions seem to have become the prerogative of tantric practitioners. The Buddha, however, was very compassionate; understanding the need of those who have no appreciation of tantric practice, he supplemented the core teachings with methods even non-Buddhists could use. Although the teachings may seem strange to a non-Buddhist, he or she needs to remember no one can escape death. The teachings explain what to expect in the bardo of becoming; upon entering there, the bardo being is prepared for what it encounters, thus minimizing fear and confusion.

The practice instructions of the six bardos contain a lot of standard Buddhist visualizations, such as of the personal deity and the guru, to which followers of other religions may be unaccustomed. It is not necessary, however, to adhere literally to the form as described. It is perfectly fine for them to replace the personal deity with a holy being of their religion, and the guru with a comparable personage from their own tradition. For example people in Macau traditionally believe in the Goddess Ama. In the bardo of becoming, the Goddess Ama can facilitate the blocking of the entrance of the womb. There is no need to investigate whether Goddess Ama really has the power or not. As long as she is considered a symbol of omniscient power and protection by the mental body, the mere thought of her in the bardo will be effective. Tantric beings are symbolic representations of purity, auspiciousness and holiness, but other holy beings are imbued with similar qualities. For the bardo being, the mere thought of holy beings will bring about the blocking of the entrance of the womb. This is because blocking the entrance of the womb depends entirely on the mental force of the bardo being; there is no Buddha or other holy being actually standing at the entrance of the womb.

From this we can see that Buddhist teachings are not mere superstitions. All that we experience is caused by our bodily, verbal and mental actions; they have the power to determine our form, our environment and our tendencies. Buddhism is training the mind; Buddhist practices can transform our ordinary confused mind and help us experience peace, serenity, equanimity and true happiness. In the bardo of becoming, the mental body has a last chance to attain such a transformation and avoid samsaric rebirth. Liberation is possible.

Visualizing a personal deity or guru is a skillful means to help the mental body generate a mind of quintessential purity and serenity. Using a symbol evoke the power of the mind to attain liberation is the thrust of the practice of the bardo of becoming. If we do not understand this, the entire practice will be twisted into a supplication for the supernatural protection. Having clarified this common misunderstanding, we can now proceed with the discussion on the six methods.

Blocking the Entrance of the Womb with our Personal Deity

Generation stage practitioners should gain familiarity with every detail of their personal deity so that his or her clear appearance will instantly arise in their mind. Being familiar with visualization of the personal deity during our lifetime will help our mental body in the bardo withstand howling whirlwinds, fierce hailstorms, attacks by angry crowds, and other terrifying experiences. If our mental body can remain calm and instantly generate itself in the clear appearance of its personal deity, then these frightening experiences will vanish. It can then easily concentrate on visualizing all naturally arisen appearances in the form of its own personal deity and his or her *mandala*. For example, if our own personal deity is Vajrasattva, then all beings in the bardo (including the mental body itself) become Vajrasattva, the entire environment becomes the *mandala* of Vajrasattva, and all sounds becomes the mantra of Vajrasattva. In order to develop this faculty of mind, we do the following visualization during the generation-stage practice. We begin by saying, "I have died and am in the bardo. All that appear are but phenomena in a bardo; all beings are beings in the bardo. Now, I must generate myself as my personal deity." After gaining a clear appearance, we then visualize all beings (even those appearing as animals) in the form of our personal deity, and we see the entire environment as his or her divine realm. Then we recite the mantra while listening closely to the sound. All other sounds we hear – the television, the door bell, traffic – are the mantra of our personal deity. We repeat this practice regularly under different environments, first in a quiet place and then in a noisy place. We can even do this practice while we are shopping or watching TV. After repeated practice, no matter where we are, we can easily recognize that all that appears is our personal deity and his or her *mandala*, and all sounds are mantra. If we do this practice until it is second nature, we will be able to recall our personal deity upon entering the bardo of becoming. The entrance of the womb will be blocked and the mental body will be naturally liberated and attain the state of Vidyadhara.

When the mental body is on the verge of taking the next rebirth (which is the last moment of the bardo of becoming), it will see male and female (human or animals) copulating. If it is going to take rebirth as a male, jealousy will arise towards the male. If it is going to take rebirth as a female, jealousy will arise towards the female. The moment jealousy (or passion) arises, the mental body enters the womb. This moment is of paramount importance because it will pass as quickly as a flash of lightening. If the mental body has not yet attained liberation at this stage, it should immediately visualize the copulating male and female as the union of its personal deity with his consort, as well as generate itself as its personal deity. As soon as it can accomplish the visualization, it can attain liberation in the streams of light of the personal deity's *mandala*.

Blocking the Entrance of the Womb with our Spiritual Guru and his Consort

Spiritual guru in this context generally refers to the Tibetan tantric master Guru Padmasambhava; his consort is Yeshe Tsogyal (Tib. *Ye shes mtsho rgyal*). Their union is commonly called the union of father and mother. In tantric imagery, many deities are depicted in a sexual embrace (in union). Many people have misunderstood this particular form of tantric representation; viewing the images of union through a lens of cultural prejudice, they see vulgar images of lust. They are very much mistaken. The union of Father and Mother, in fact, has many deep meanings: fundamentally, it symbolizes the infinite displays of vitality pervading all dimensions of time and space, permeating all of samsara and nirvana. What can be a better symbol of vitality than the sacred union of male and female? If we do not realize naturally arisen phenomena through observing their infinite vitality pervading space, then our scope of understanding will be narrowly constrained. We may even get stuck with its literal meaning and become nihilistic. Under proper guidance, realizing the vitality pervading space is the best method to realize the aspect of infinite displays.

In generation-stage practice, we imagine ourselves as the bardo being about to be drawn into the womb. At that critical moment, we generate as our personal deity and visualize the union of Guru Padmasambhava and his consort. We request them to grant us the empowerment. Instantaneously, the entrance of the womb is closed. To succeed in blocking the entrance of the womb through this visualization method, we need to be experienced with guru yoga or generation stage practice. There is a difference between visualizing the union of our guru with his consort and visualizing the union of our personal deity with his consort. In the former, the mental body is the disciple and it requests his guru to grant the empowerment; in the latter, the mental body generates itself as the personal deity (it can be solitary or in union). Which method we adopt depends very much on our faculty. Each has its own merits. If the mental body had no experience in generation-stage practice while it was alive, it may not be easy to generate itself as a deity or holy being. In this case, visualizing its guru and his consort will be more beneficial.

It is not absolutely necessary for a tantric practitioner in the bardo of becoming to visualize Guru Padmasambhava and his consort. As long as the mental body maintains a pure mind of faith and respect, and transform all its thoughts into pure thoughts, the entrance of the womb will be blocked. If it has no knowledge of experience in tantric practices, it can visualize the sages of its religion blocking the entrance of the womb. The most important thing is to purify all jealousy and desire, and maintain a mind of purity. Once the mind of faith arises, the goal will be attained.

Blocking the Entrance of the Womb by Generating the Four (States of) Bliss

This method is suitable only for tantric practitioners who are familiar with

completion-stage practice. In fact, for an accomplished completion-stage practitioner, there is no need to go through the stage of blocking the entrance of the
womb. During the dissolution of the earth, water, fire and wind in the death
process, the red drop of the mother ascends up the central channel while the
white drop of the father descends to the heart channel wheel. When the two
meet, infinite lively displays of red and white drops manifest, and great bliss
arises. After the gross wind enters the central channel but before the inner wind
ceases, an accomplished completion-stage practitioner, relying on the practice of
the four (states of) bliss done during his or her lifetime generates great bliss in
order to cause the primordial wisdom to arise – the union of bliss and emptiness.
Upon the realization of this wisdom, liberation is instantaneously attained. These
instructions must be practiced under the close guidance of a qualified guru. You
should never attempt tantric practices relating to the union of father and mother
by merely relying on books. If done incorrectly, these practices not only cause
problems in this life, but can also cause ejaculation (male or female) during the
dying process and lead to a lower rebirth.

If liberation is not attained in the bardo of dying, we can try to attain liberation in the bardo of *dharmata* through visualizing the peaceful or wrathful deities
in the union of father and mother. For an experienced practitioner, great bliss
arises from such visualization, and primordial wisdom subsequently manifests.
Liberation is attained.

In the bardo of dying, a practitioner with inferior faculties cannot spontaneously realize the four (states of) bliss in the same way that a practitioner with
superior faculty can. In the bardo of *dharmata*, neither can it spontaneously realize the aspect of cognizance and infinite displays in the same way a practitioner
of middling faculty can The practitioner with inferior faculties has no choice but
to attain liberation in the bardo of becoming by transforming into great bliss the
desire that arises when it sees male and female copulating. Through it attaining
the union of bliss and emptiness, the entrance of the womb is blocked.

Blocking the Entrance of the Womb
with the Antidote of Renunciation

The practice of generating bliss through the union of male and female is not
an appropriate method for ordained monks and nuns who have taken the vow of
celibacy. In this case, when they see father and mother copulating in the bardo,
they should immediately generate the mind of renunciation as an antidote to

their grasping toward the forms appearing before them. When their passion or ordinary conception towards the copulating male and female abates, the entrance of the womb will be blocked; they will take a fortunate rebirth. Although this method is inferior to the preceding methods that we have just explained, it has can be easily applied by those who have taken a vow of celibacy. Those who do not keep vows can maintain a natural mind as an antidote to their overwhelming passion. When desire and jealously abate, they can attain a fortunate rebirth based on their good karma.

Blocking the Entrance of the Womb with the Clear Light
Blocking the Entrance of the Womb with the Illusory Body

These two methods are not suitable for ordinary people. In order to apply the former method successfully, the mental body had to have experience with the practice of clear light, *trekcho* or *thogal*, while it is alive. For the latter method, the mental body has to at least have experience with dream yoga before the entrance of the womb can be blocked to attain liberation. Therefore, we will not elaborate on these two methods here.

The key points of the essential practices of the bardo of becoming are as follows:

- A generation-stage practitioner should recognize the nature of all appearing forms, all phenomena, of the bardo of living in the form its personal deity with its consort or his or her guru with his consort. In other words, the practice is to realize the aliveness of all phenomena pervading space through their infinite displays.
- A completion-stage practitioner should recognize all appearances as cognizance. That mean it recognizes all appearances as the naturally arisen primordial wisdom, which naturally-arises from emptiness itself.
- All appearances are like mirror reflections. Although they appear, they do not inherently exist. They appear, but yet are empty; we call it appearance-emptiness.
- In the bardo of dreams, we try to recognize the deceptiveness of daytime appearances and the illusiveness of dream appearances.
- From recognizing how illusory and deceptive these appearances are, infinite displays and clear light of purity occur. The

basis of attaining liberation in the bardo is grounded on such realization.

Practitioners should practice after the meditation session in the following way:

- We visualize all that appear are but naturally arisen phenomena we see while wandering in the bardo upon our death.
- We regard all beings that are born, or not yet born, as bardo beings in the bardo of becoming.
- We then visualize all phenomena, thunder and lightning, rain and snow, bustling crowds, growling dogs, people going about their business, as phenomena in the bardo, elusive and transient.
- We recognize what we considered to be solidly real in our life is, in fact, illusive and transitory, just like a phenomenon in a bardo. This is the state of the bardo of becoming.
- We recognize all our friends and relatives existing in this transitory state, as if they have already died, and are just like us, roaming in the bardo.
- After repeated practice, we eventually attain the realization of *Mahamudra*. When our mind can habitually abide in this state, we are able to attain liberation in the bardo of *dharmata*.
- We always abide the mind in the naturally arisen state, uncontrived and without elaboration. When thoughts arise, we dissolve them into the four liberating states.
- We realize that all phenomena are naturally arising and naturally liberating. This is the state of the bardo of meditation.
- We maintain this state of mind after formal meditation sessions. If we can always abide our mind in the primordial purity, then we will be able to realize the clear light of death and attain liberation in the bardo of dying.

The above are the key points of the practices. If we can relate the first three bardos, which we practice during our lifetime, to the last three bardos, which we practice at the moment of death and after death, then it is very easy to understand how liberation is attained.

CONCLUSION

The Three States of Meditative Absorption

*N*ATURAL *APPEARANCES, NATURAL LIBERATION* is so titled to remind us that liberation can be attained in any of the bardos, both during our lifetime as well as upon our death. It is written specifically to review the intent of the profound esoteric doctrine of this Nyingma terma. To gain a deep insight into the essence of this esoteric teaching, we have to read this book as a whole and weave out the intricacies of the relationships between the bardos of our lifetime and the bardos upon our death.

In our lifetime, the practice of the bardo of living is associated with the bardo of becoming; the practice of the bardo of dreams is associated with the bardo of *dharmata*; the practice of the bardo of meditation is associated with the bardo of dying. Upon our death, attaining liberation in the bardo of dying depends very much on our how experienced we are with the practice of the bardo of meditation during our lifetime. Similarly, attaining liberation in the bardo of *dharmata* depends very much on how experienced we are with the practice of the bardo of meditation. Similarly, in the bardo of becoming, attaining liberation depends on our familiarity (how experienced we are) with the practice of the bardo of living. Although this pairing may seem a bit contrived (as all practices are inter-related), such arrangement is intended to correlate the three groups of practices with the three aspects of all naturally arisen phenomena – emptiness, cognizance, and in-finite displays.

I must remind readers that naturally arisen appearance is very different from appearance itself. When we see an appearance, we are using our mind to ap-prehend it. All that appears pass through the distorted lens of our mind. When we refer to naturally arisen appearance, however, our mind acts like a mirror. It will reflect whatever that falls on it. This reflection is naturally arisen, without any mental contrivances or conceptual imputations. We are not denying the validity of conceptual imputation; we are just saying that if we impute any concepts over and above how things should be, we will not be able to recognize their true nature. That is why we call them distortions of the mind. Whatever kinds of distortions are, they are mental constraints, hindrances to liberation.

How can we realize naturally arisen phenomena? Emptiness is the nature of all naturally arisen phenomena, cognizance is their appearance, and their infinite displays are their inherent capability or faculty. We have to realize these three aspects simultaneously, before we can be considered to have attained the spontaneous realization of naturally arisen phenomena.

The Nyingma tradition does not recommend that the practitioner realize emptiness according to a set of preconceived definitions. Realizing a set of concepts from another set of concepts is only a process of distorted mental actions. In our practice, therefore, we need to realize the nature of phenomena and how it naturally arises through the appearances and functions of those phenomena. The key to realizing infinite displays lies in recognizing aliveness pervading space, while the key to realizing cognizance lies on recognizing its appearances. Permeating infinite aliveness is a capability inherent in all phenomena or things while appearances are their outer expressions. Realizing them both, we can then realize what emptiness is. This aspect of emptiness is the nature of all things.

Among the practices in the six bardos, the bardo of living and the bardo of becoming both emphasize the aspect of infinite displays, that is, realizing the aliveness pervading space. The bardo of dreams and the bardo of *dharmata* both emphasize the aspect of cognizance that is, realizing its manifestations (generally referred to as clear light). The bardo of meditation and the bardo of dying both emphasize the aspect of emptiness.

The nature, appearance and function of all things are inseparable. Although the practices of the six bardos are divided into three major sections, the teachings should be understood in their entirety. In other words, when we attain natural liberation in the bardo of dying through realizing emptiness from the clear light of death, such realization is not separate from the realization of its appearances and aliveness. Similarly, when we attain natural liberation in the bardo of *dharmata* through realizing cognizance from the appearances of the peaceful and wrathful deities, such realization is not separate from the realization of emptiness and aliveness. By the same token, when we attain natural liberation in the bardo of becoming through realizing the aspect of infinite displays from the aliveness pervading space, we must have also simultaneously realized emptiness and its appearances. Once we understand the intricacies among their relationships, we can envision the unity of living and dying, and how nature, appearance and function should be viewed in its entirety.

Whether we are in the bardo of dying, the bardo of *dharmata*, or the bardo of becoming, everything that appears is but the naturally arisen display of *dharmata*.

The clear light of death is the naturally arisen display of *dharmata*. The lights, the flashes the deafening noise, the peaceful and wrathful deities are the naturally arisen displays of *dharmata*. The scenes that appear of male and female copulating are also the naturally arisen displays of *dharmata*, and so are those of the six realms. If the mental body can spontaneously realize that all phenomena are naturally arising, the body will be naturally liberated because it has cleared away all the distortions of the mind-itself. Upon that moment of realization, our innate clear light will naturally arise.

It is, however, difficult for the mental body to attain that realization precisely because it is part of the naturally arisen *dharmata*. It is analogous to the people we watch on television; they do not realize that their appearances are deceptive and illusory because they are part of the illusion. While we watch, we may also be taken in by the illusion. But when we turn off the program, we instantly realize all that appear on the screens are mere illusions. Living in this mundane world of ours, we encounter the same difficulties. To use an analogy we have used before, being a part of this mundane world is like being an appearance on a television screen. Because we are part of the illusion, we do not recognize how deceptive all its appearances are.

The teachings in this commentary provide us a framework of instructions in realizing the naturally arisen phenomena. Methodologically, it is analogous to the example of the people appearing on the television screen. When their minds are liberated from the constraints of the screen, even though they are still appearing on screen, they will be able to recognize instantly that all that appears is mere illusion. When the mind moves away from the screen, it enters into meditative absorption – an uninterrupted concentration. Upon this spontaneous realization, their emotional state is transformed. The same holds true for ourselves: even though we are still appearing on the screen of mundane existence, our outlook is different because we have extensive experience on how delusive and deceptive appearances are. When we abide in this state, we rest in the mind-itself.

We then extend the screen of our world to all realms. We extend the scope of the naturally arisen phenomena recognized by the mind-itself to all naturally arisen displays, including those that the mind-itself does not recognize, such as nirvana. When this mind abides in the *dharmata* this way, it is naturally liberated. The moment our mind enters into this state of meditative absorption is the instance we attain such spontaneous realization. When our mind continuously abides in this luminous absorption, it illuminates our daily activities and allows us to live in a heightened state of mental awareness. Although our mind is constantly abiding in this heightened state, it is not rigid like stone. It still experiences the ups and downs of life, but these fluctuations no longer influence our psychological state. We are like a tree of which the roots remain firm even while the branches sway in the wind. The state of meditative absorption permeates all moments of our lives.

Some traditions regard the natural liberation of the mind-itself (which simultaneously abides in *dharmata*) to be the ultimate realization. From the Nyingma's point of view, however, the mind-itself abiding in *dharmata* is only a stage of liberation because the mind is still within the horizon of *dharmata*, abiding in an attributed state of purity.

In the *Vimalakirti-nidesa* (the Holy Teachings of Vimalakirti), when Brahma Sikhin saw the Buddha-field of Buddha Shakyamuni (i.e. our world), he immediately recognized its purity because his mind-itself was liberated. Shariputra saw the same emanation but he regarded it to be defiled and confused because of the non-liberated state of his mind. Although Brahma Sikhin had not yet attained full enlightenment, his mind waited patiently in the *dharmata* and thus the mind-itself was pure. Since his mind was pure, whatever appeared to him was also be pure. However, this purity is precisely what bound his mind. The Buddha-fields, whether pure or impure, are all displayed unfettered, without any restraints. This is the natural liberation of *dharmata*. When *dharmata* is naturally liberated, the mind abides in equanimity. In such state, there is no difference between pure land and defiled land; nirvana and samsara are the same. The moment the mind abides in equanimity is the moment one enters into such meditative absorption. This is "natural mind."

Abiding in equanimity does not mean that everything is the same as everything else. It does not mean that everyone looks the same, that all sounds sound the same, or that all tastes taste the same. Abiding in equanimity is a state that transcends time and space, which has been the object of our innate grasping since beginning-less time. Our timeline is always moving in one direction from past to present to future, and the space around us always has three dimensions. That is why even our concept of Buddha is imbued with the flavor of the three times: the Buddha of the past, present and future. That is why the statues of the Buddha and temples we have built are always three-dimensional. This is neither natural mind nor the nature of equanimity. When the mind abides in the state of equanimity, it is far beyond the constraints of time and space. In a sutra it says, "To recognize all worlds, all realms, the way they are." The phrase suggests a state which transcends time and space. Otherwise, how can it say "all worlds, all realms"?

The state of meditative absorption is the state of the transformation of the mind. The mind transforms progressively and abides correspondingly in its progressive states. Hence, natural liberation occurs in progressive stages. We have not discussed the natural liberation of equanimity because abiding in equanimity and naturally liberated from its horizon have very subtle differences which are difficult to articulate in words. In the *Maharatnakuta Sutra*, there is a conversation between Sarthavahadevaputra and Bodhisattva Manjushri:

> Sarthavahadevaputra asks, "Manjushri, how can I realize the phenomena of samsara?"
>
> Manjushri answers, "Knowing that all phenomena arise from the interdependent relationship of causes and effects, and knowing that they are not perpetuating nor interrupting, then you know all about samsara."
>
> Sarthavahadevaputra asks, "What is the definition of samsara?"
>
> Manjushri answers, "Samsara is *dharmadhatu*."
>
> Sarthavahadevaputra asks, "What is *dharmadhatu*?"
>
> Manjushri answers, "*Dharmadhatu* is the realm empty of inherent existence."
>
> Sarthavahadevaputra asks, "What is the realm of emptiness?"
>
> Manjushri answers, "When it transcends all states, it is the realm of emptiness."
>
> Sarthavahadevaputra asks, "What is this transcended state like?"
>
> Manjushri answers, "It is the state of the Buddha,"
>
> Sarthavahadevaputra asked, "What is the state of the Buddha?"
>
> Manjushri answers, "Eye element is the state of Buddha; however, the state of Buddha is not the eye, or the visual sight, or the state of eye consciousness. Ear element is the state of the Buddha; however, the state of Buddha is not the ear, or the auditory sound, or the state of ear consciousness. Similarly, our mind element is the state of the Buddha; however, the state of Buddha is not the mind, or the mental form, or the state of mental consciousness. Form element is the state of the Buddha, but the state of Buddha is not the state of form. Feeling, perception, mental formation, and consciousness are the states of Buddha, yet the states of Buddha are not the states of feeling, perception, motivation and consciousness. Delusion element is the state of the Buddha;

nevertheless, the state of the Buddha is not the state of delusion. Thus, aging, sickness, and death elements are the state of the Buddha; however, the state of the Buddha is not the state of aging, sickness, and death. The desire realm is the state of the Buddha because it is devoid of the expression of desire. Form realm is the state of the Buddha because it is not for the elimination of desire. Formless realm is the state of the Buddha because there is no delusion. The non-volition realm is the state of the Buddha because there is no dualistic appearance. Conditioned realm is the state of the Buddha because it does not have three appearances (past, present, future). Sarthavahadevaputra, these are the states of the Buddha. These states exist in all realms. It does not matter if they are finite or infinite; they are inclusively the states of *dharmadhatu*. Understand the state of Buddha and the state of *Mara* just as they are. Know that they are peaceful and equal. This is the most powerful miraculous ability. Moreover, bodhisattvas do not abide in equanimity but ripen the sentient beings through the means of equanimity."

This sutra has summarized the main tenet of the teachings. "Samsara is *dharmadhatu*" is realized when the mind-itself is naturally liberated and simultaneously abides in *dharmata*. "*Dharmadhatu* is the state of emptiness which transcends all states" is realized when *dharmata* is naturally liberated and simultaneously abides in equanimity. The state of Buddha is not separated, however, from the eyes, ears, nose, tongue, body, mind, form, feeling, perception, mental formation and consciousness in samsara. Only when this is realized, natural liberation of equanimity is attained. At this stage, not even the concept of equanimity exists. At this stage, all constraints are liberated. If we have to articulate this state in words, we can marginally say that this state no longer abides in equanimity but performs meritorious deeds through the means of equanimity. It is "neither the same nor different," "neither one nor separate."

Under the constraints of our aggregates, bases and elements, it is a remarkable achievement to attain natural liberation of *dharmata* and abide in the state of equanimity. When we realize that state, we are already bodhisattvas on the tenth ground. It is rather difficult to attain Buddhahood. The six bardos provide us with a framework for practice so that we can take advantage of the moment when the mind is not bound under its innate constraints, to attain liberation. The last three bardos are geared specifically to make use of the three special opportunities upon death. Although it is not an easy task, it is comparatively easier than attaining natural liberation during our lifetime. For added insurance, the method of transference of consciousness is also included in the teachings.

The stage of blocking the entrance of the womb in the bardo of becoming is the last opportunity to attain liberation. If the mental body does not succeed in blocking the entrance of the womb, it will have to take rebirth once again in samsara. At this stage, all it can do is to seek for a virtuous womb to take rebirth. For a tantric practitioner who is seeking for a virtuous womb to take rebirth, his mental body must remember to first take refuge in the three jewels, confess its non-virtuous deeds and then generate itself in the form of its personal deity. Further, it should generate the aspiration to benefit other sentient beings in its emergent life. Through such virtuous intent, all non-virtuous wombs will be blocked; the mental body will eventually enter a virtuous womb for rebirth. This means the mental body will be reborn with a healthy body and mind in a suitable family where there will be sufficient resources for her to meet with and practise the Dharma. She will meet and be guided by good teachers of the Dharma and in turn bestow the teachings to others and lead them onto the path.

For the non-Buddhist, his mental body should also confess his wrongdoings while recalling all the virtuous deeds in his lifetime. Then his mental body must remember to generate the wish to enter a virtuous womb to take rebirth so that it can benefit other beings in its emergent life.

Liberation through the six bardos not only contains very practical teachings, but also has embedded in it many teachings of the Nyingma tantric tradition, especially the Dharma Gate of non-duality and the Dharma Gate of the inconceivability. Since its teachings transcend dualistic phenomena, it is a Dharma of non-duality. Since it is based on inner realization of our innate wisdom, it is a Dharma of inconceivability.

This text is not intended as a study of spiritualism or psychology. Neither is it intended to be viewed as handbook for taking care of the deceased or a treatise on emptiness. The intention is to condense the very deep and profound tantric teachings into practices approachable by all sentient beings so that many can swiftly attain liberation. If we practice unwaveringly, spontaneous realization will come, and liberation is certain.

May this teaching continue to bring benefits to all sentient beings until samsara has been emptied. May all be auspicious!

Translator's Postscript

I have been honored to have had the opportunity to translate Master Tam Shek-wing's commentary on one of the important hidden-treasure teachings discovered by Terton Karma Lingpa of the Nyingma Lineage. Master Tam's commentary, written in Chinese, was first published as a series of articles for general readership in the *Hong Kong Economic Journal* in 2000; the articles were published in book form in 2005.

Master Tam is not only a realized meditation master but also an exceptionally talented writer. He possesses laser-sharp perception that can penetrate all levels of his students' minds, down to their core being. Endowed with enormous insights and creativity, he always encourages his students to be who they are and to develop their own unique expressions in life. He encouraged me to put his text in my own words and style. It was his inspiring vision that made completing this translated text possible.

Translating Master Tam's commentary was itself a process of awakening. It not only gave me tremendous insight into the topic, but opened my mind to a broad spectrum of knowledge drawn from disciplines such as philosophical Daoism and Chinese Chan Buddhism. The vivid, yet sophisticated meditative insights in the commentary lead me to an intense meditative experience while working on the translation. I also compared commentaries written at different times by different masters; through researching different perspectives, I began to appreciate the versatility of the original text and the profundity of the doctrine. Like rainbows in the sky, the expressions from each master so rich and uniquely different from one another, are yet able to inspire us through their unique experiences and insights.

In being translated into English, Master Tam's text was amended to suit Western tastes; while not a word-for-word translation, the English text nonetheless faithfully conveys Master Tam's original meaning and intention. The commentary reveals the path to natural liberation based on the profound doctrine of the Great Madhyamaka, from the view of the Great Perfection (Dzogchen) of the Nyingma Lineage. Master Tam has a unique light-hearted way of explaining deep philosophical issues using down-to-earth examples from daily life, to which general readers can very easily relate. However, Master Tam cautions us that analogies are only analogies; they are not intended to be analyzed critically; their purpose is to inspire readers to connect with the meaning of the text. To illustrate, Master

Tam told us an ancient Buddhist story: A disciple once asked his master, "What is white?" The master replied, "White is like the colour of a (white) swan." Then the disciple replied, "Oh, white must then have feathers." The master shook his head and sighed, "The colour of snow is also white." The disciple immediately replied, "Ah, white must be cold." The master shook his head again, and said, "White is the colour of conch shells." The disciple mulled over the master's replies, and suddenly exclaimed, "Yes, I understand now. The colour white lives by the seashore, has feathers and is cold. That is the osprey right down the shore! So the black osprey becomes a living thing called white."

I am grateful to Master Tam, Agnes Cheng, Beverley Giblon, Sandra Monteath, John Negru, Jenny Tang, Ed Lui, and Henry Shiu for their help in making this book available in the present form.

The wisdom state of the Buddha cannot be explained. It is an inconceivable inner realization beyond words and elaborations. The purpose of this commentary is to inspire general readers to get onto the path to attain full liberation. May it accomplish its purpose and inspire many to swiftly attain liberation.

Samten Migdron

Born into an affluent family in Hong Kong, Samten Migdron has been a dharma practitioner since 1995. She holds a BA in Liberal Studies and an MA in Finance and has also completed the Advanced Management Program at Harvard Business School. Although she has a successful career in finance and management, Samten Migdron is at heart a poet, an artist, a meditator, a healer and a progressive thinker.

She experienced her first spiritual awakening in 1995 shortly after she started practising Tibetan Buddhism. Since then, she has dedicated herself to meditation, Buddhist studies, yoga, healing and astrology to explore the nature of mind and reality. She has received numerous transmissions and esoteric teachings in the Mahamudra and Dzogchen tradition. Currently, Samten Migdron resides in Hong Kong, and hosts occasional workshops relating to mind and consciousness.